THE USE OF THE PSALMS

FOR
SPIRITUAL AND
EMOTIONAL GROWTH

DAVID J. BICK

THE USE OF THE PSALMS

FOR
SPIRITUAL AND
EMOTIONAL GROWTH

by

DAVID J. BICK

Excalibur Press of London
13 Knightsbridge Green, London SW1X 7QL

Published by Excalibur Press of London
Typesetting by CBS Felixstowe Suffolk
ISBN 1 85634 117 8

With contributions by Mary J Ratzer who also did the supporting research for this work.

CONTENTS

Psalm 54(55) for those who have been let down by a close
friend

INTRODUCTION

Psalm Numbering & Versions

More than two centuries before Christ, in Alexandria, the psalms were translated into Greek. This version, known as the Septuagint version, was used by the early church for the preaching of Christianity; it served as the basis for the earliest translations, particularly the Latin translation (known as the Vulgate) which was used widely in the Church. In recent times, with the progress in Biblical studies, the translations are usually made directly from the original Hebrew texts.

The numbering of the psalms found in most International Christian liturgies is taken from the Greek Septuagint; the numeration differs from that found in the Hebrew text (and in the Authorised version). The numbering of the verses is also slightly different in the different translations. The traditional liturgical texts usually include the title of the psalm in the body of the text; whereas the more recent translations tend to exclude the title when numbering the verses.

In this work, a translation from the Hebrew is used in which special attention was paid to the rhythmic structure of the poetry of the psalms. The numbering follows the International liturgical (Greek) system with the Hebrew number following in brackets; the verse numbering also follows the liturgical system.

The Framework of This Book

The whole of this work could be seen as an exposition of the meaning of the Parable of the Good Samaritan (the Gospel of Luke 10:29-39). It does not claim to be a complete exposition, but an exposition of an important point the parable makes that can be observed by any aware Pastor as being continually perpetuated by certain institutions of the Christian Church in each of its denominations.

The point made is a simple one. It is that the inflexible disciplines of some religious institutions can render people incapable of making an honest response to situations in life that demand a demonstration of God's love. This, in turn, can lead to an inability to make a full and honest response to God. It seems that in this parable, Jesus is saying that certain types of rigid legalistic and heavily moralistic religious training and discipline can destroy people's actual living faith, rendering them empty, spiritually impotent and cut off from God. In the parable, the priest and Levite, both strictly disciplined and trained religious people, were like this; whereas the Samaritan who was despised for his lack of these things, was the one able to make the 'good neighbour' response to the situation. There are other instances in the gospels where Jesus takes this stance against the legalistic religious institutions of his time.

Many people in the modern world fall into the same general category as the Samaritan. They are often puzzled by 'theological niceties' and 'ecclesiastical protocol'. They desire God and a spiritual dimension to their lives but remain unsatisfied by what the official structures of the churches offer them.

This is an invitation to such people to look again (from a vantage point outside these 'official' religious structures) at what is offered in the scriptures, and especially within the Psalms, and by so doing to make an individual but honest response to what God could be saying through them. Perhaps Jesus Christ himself is saying this to many people now. From how he is portrayed in the four Gospels, he was very much on the fringe or even outside the official priestly institutions of his day; but at the same time well within the established spiritual tradition of a prophetic kind, within the body of believers.

In any study done from a vantage point outside the main stream religious structures, it is important that we do not fall into the trap of thinking we have, in some way, a superior knowledge; that we are, in some way, in a better position to 'understand these hidden things' about life. In our study of psychology and the various therapies, it is important that our thought does not degenerate into a neo-gnostic therapeutic framework. Though Christ himself seemingly takes an outside stance vis-à-vis the established religious order of his day, he had indeed a knowledge of 'hidden things' (gnosis), and in that sense he alone truly had the right (though he did not exercise it) to stand apart and take a wholly objective stance. It must not be forgotten that Christ took into account our human frailty and need for group support; in his dealings with his early followers he supplied them with that very support he knew we needed. In the presence of his followers, he addressed Peter:

"I tell you, you are Peter*, and upon this rock I will build my church"

[*Petros = rock]   Matthew 16:18

Throughout the history of the church that Christ founded for our help and support, there have been those who have been unable to cope with the hurly-burly of human contact within the Church, with the warmth and the conflict inherent in that contact; they have taken an 'outsider's' view. These seekers after the truth about life and death, have in their inability to muck in with ordinary Christian folk, become aloof, in their superior knowledge.

> "The gnostic assumes he knows better than the record of the witnesses (even the biblical ones) because he feels his own independent mental aristocracy is an endowment which takes precedence over mere evidence in the objective world. Gnostics show disdain, and not a little bitterness, towards ordinary Christian folk, who love their life in the world as God gave it to them. This reveals something of the secret scorn of themselves into which they were driven. It conceals and denies their deep envy of warm human ties, against the acceptance of which their life is in recoil."
> [*Clinical Theology*. Frank Lake. DLT 1986]

The response invited in this study is a full one, not just at an intellectual level. Our emotions must also be engaged. For many, this is not easy because today's educational process conditions us to ignore them. As a result they often become distorted and seriously affect intellectual judgements, causing us much agony that is often dressed up as intellectual problems of faith. The Psalms are amongst the most emotionally honest and direct of all the scriptures. They tend at times to offend our intellectual sense of decency. Perhaps this is the reason why the Anglican prayer book has some parts bracketed out, phrases which are important expressions of human pain.

As we grow in personal spirituality and psychological health, we will discover that the road is not straight but characterised by heights and depths. We discover that at some points we feel the need to protect our fragile inner self by silence and protective withdrawal; at other times we feel the need to grow by communicating with another. Most of the time we jog along a comfortable path between inner anxiety and outward insecurity, we keep behind our masks. It is only when the equilibrium is threatened that we dare to reveal ourselves to the other and seek one who can hear what we are unable to say and one who can see what we do not dare look at. If we avoid the commitment to dialogue we remain in defensive isolation.

The aim in writing is not to produce a study of the psalms, but to use some of the psalms as a vehicle for helping people to recognise, accept and cope with their difficult emotions. Only certain psalms will be used and these will be selected because the emotions they express to God are relevant to certain types of personality and certain kinds of human situations. The study will be deliberately limited to those things that relate to the emotional and spiritual health of individuals.

The framework will be:

#1   Firstly to say something about human nature and the human predicament, and then to set out with brief description an outline of the types of defenses we use to cope with the more threatening aspects of our daily lives.

#2   Secondly, certain psalms will be selected and related to each general kind of defense people take in an attempt to deal with their emotional pain.

#3   Thirdly, a section will be based upon certain human predicaments and psalms selected to fit them, including some affirmative Psalms.

The reader is invited to assess which type of defense mechanism applies to them, and then choose relevant psalms for meditation and prayer. It is therefore suggested that the best use of this book is firstly to read it all to gain an overall understanding, and then use just relevant psalms for meditation in any given situation.

Finally, from this one could move on to other psalms not mentioned and thereby build up a practical method for using the psalms based upon our own individual personality and needs. This is nothing new; for centuries many faithful people of the Judeo-Christian tradition have used the psalms as spiritual food, both in liturgy and in personal prayer.

CHAPTER 1:1

HUMAN NATURE: SIN & EVIL

- The Human Predicament and Human Nature -

Life as we experience it here on earth is not rational. It is at best full of contradictions and at worst meaningless. The human struggle over the centuries as expressed in art, music, literature, religion and philosophy adequately illustrates this point. Nobody seems to have found the 'answer'; at least, not a universal one. Many think they have found it for themselves, but then others expose its inadequacies for them. One sets up a hypothesis for another to knock down. In such a manner is the intellectual game played. I call it a game because at one level it is, but I do not deny that behind it lies a serious attempt to make life meaningful. This 'making meaningful' though pursued intellectually has behind it a powerful emotional thrust which in turn points to a deep emotional need. This is why all are engaged in making their own personal life meaningful, but only a few enter into the intellectual game of attempting to impose a rationality onto life. The majority just jog along in a very basic 'hand to mouth' survival routine and for most of these thinking is too painful, fruitless for the achievement of happiness, or just beyond them.

It is therefore the intellectuals who expose this deeply rooted problem of the irrationality of life. It is they who seem to feel strongly that somehow it must be rational and to make it so would be the 'answer'. I say 'feel' here rather than 'think', because behind all intellectual activity there must be some emotional drive to motivate it, for intellect alone is sterile and unproductive. The use of the intellect in this kind of problem solving, or exercise for giving meaning, is not of itself a bad or negative thing. It can indeed be very helpful; but before engaging in it one must be able to recognise its limitations. They are that human intellect does not represent the whole of our humanity or the world in which we live. A large part of our world of experience is purely emotional. This world of emotion has its own logic which from an intellectual viewpoint appears so devious and powerful that it can dominate us causing us to fear it. An even larger part of our experience is spiritual and beyond intellectual understanding. This is a mysterious world to be understood or perceived only by those who would make a total response to it and not just an intellectual one. It is the mystery and vastness of the spiritual world that frightens many, as does the emotional part of us which, if not understood and properly expressed, can so easily dominate and enslave. Therefore from the motivation of fear, many are driven to seal these two worlds off in safe intellectual boxes.

The key issue then, about which we now concern ourselves is our response to our predicament of having to live in a world which we can only partly control or understand. Eventually I intend to look at this response and its implications as expressed in the psalms, but before doing this more must be said about it in general terms.

There are three general principles which would seem to determine our response. Firstly, it must be total, that is within the totality of ourselves. Secondly, the grace of God must play its part; and thirdly, an adequate understanding of sin and evil is essential.

- 1: A total response

This involves the spiritual, emotional and intellectual facets of the person, at the level of completeness in which they exist in him or her at the time of the response. Nobody can give what they do not have; but we can all deny or hold back that which we do have. We learn about God by responding to him in the fullest way possible for us. The atheist who shouts out: 'You do not exist', in fact affirms God's existence by so doing. The honest and positive aspect of true atheism is what the individual atheist says about his or her own personality. Atheism is a very emotional and spiritual statement about such inner emptiness and spiritual pain that life does not appear to have any ultimate meaning. It can be a total response for some people, within their present condition; but if this is so, it is most probable that sooner or later, by the grace of God, the condition will change.

I use this one illustration because it is an extreme one. Everyone needs the inner honesty and self awareness of this example so that they can respond totally from their true condition whatever it might be at any one time. Anything less is a false piety that destroys real faith. True faith does not see oneself as in control and needing to protect God or even defend faith. God and faith defend themselves when realistically viewed. It is much more healthy therefore, in our response, to express our lack with a good degree of abandonment, if we do not find such an attitude too frightening. Our growth as a whole person can come only when our nasty and negative side is accepted as a valid part of us which cannot be hidden for ever.

The life of faith is a reckless adventure at times for which those who would enter upon it need much pastoral support and encouragement. When total response is achieved it may lead many into areas of shame, therefore love and not condemnation of each other is the only way; the way of Christ as he shows us in the Gospels, and not as others may have interpreted it for themselves.

> "Judge not, that you be not judged. For with the judgement you pronounce you will be judged, and the measure you give will be the measure you get. Why do you see the speck that is in your brother's eye, but do not notice the log that is in your own eye? Or how can you say to your brother, 'Let me take the speck out of your eye,' when there is the log in your own eye? You hypocrite, first take the log out of your own eye, and then you will see clearly to take the speck out of your brother's eye."
>
> *Matthew* 7:1-5 [RSV]

- 2:   The Grace of God

This is very mysterious in the sense that like God it cannot be satisfactorily defined because it is beyond our intellectual grasp. It can however be experienced.   Its essence is only fully experienced when we are in a state of genuine humility, when we are fully aware of ourselves as we really are, without any denial of our human frailty.   There seem to be two extreme ways in which people experience grace personally.   At the highest or most dramatic level it is experienced at those times in our lives when by no virtue of our own, everything conspires to come right for us.   At the other extreme, the lowest level, it is experienced by us as having just survived against all odds, in such a way that leaves us free and able to enter fully into life at the present moment.   An example of the experience of grace at its most basic level is the following prayer from the beginning of the Passover Haggadah:

> "Blessed are you, O Lord our God, King of the Universe, who has kept us in life, sustained us, and brought us to this appointed time."

At its highest level grace is shown in deep religious experiences that give us a definite awareness of God, or transform the mundane into something transcendent and marvellous. The basic characteristic of grace is that it just happens to us. It cannot easily be defined, or gained in any way by merit or our own efforts, and we as human beings have no control over it. Grace keeps the world going despite the frailty of people and often is operative when as far as our rational skills are concerned nothing can be done at all. It is by grace alone that an honest and total response to God is possible at all on the part of any human being.

-3:   An adequate understanding of Sin and Evil
Most people have a concept of sin that is too narrow and predominantly legalistic. This is not a true reflection of Scripture.

- The Concept of Sin & Evil -

The psalms are set in the wider context of Scripture as a whole, and cannot be understood without reference to what is contained in them. One important concept that runs throughout Scripture, and is a key idea in both Jewish and Christian faith, is that of Sin. The following two prayers, one from the Jewish liturgy and one given to us by Jesus and repeated in the Christian liturgy, show how central the concept of sin is.

> "May it be thy will, O Lord my God and God of my fathers, to deliver me this day and every day from shamelessness and shameless men, from an evil man, an evil companion and an evil neighbour, and from an evil occurrence: from the corrupting tempter, and from an unjust judgement and an unjust opponent, be he a son of the covenant or be he not a son of the covenant."

> "Our Father in Heaven, hallowed be your name. Your kingdom come, your will be done on earth as it is in Heaven. Give us this day our daily bread and forgive us our trespasses as we forgive them who trespass against us. And cause us not to be lead into temptation, but deliver us from evil."

The first prayer speaks of 'shamelessness', 'evil men and occurrences', 'unjust opponents'; the second prayer speaks of 'trespasses'; both prayers speak of 'the tempter' or 'temptation' and of 'evil'.

What therefore is 'sin'? The two prayers reflect both the cosmic view of evil and the particular view of sins committed by persons. I will begin with a cosmic view.

The Judaeo-Christian attempt at an explanation of this state of cosmic imperfection is to be found in the book of *Genesis* chapter 3, starting:

> "Now the serpent was more subtle than any other wild creature that the Lord God had made ......"

Here we get our first introduction to the Devil as the serpent, the 'prompter to evil'. There is no doubt from the story that the 'prompter to evil' was part of God's creation, something made by his hands.

Satan, the 'prompter to evil', is seen as standing in the rôle of Accuser, before God he accuses man of his deeds. In the *Apocalypse* (Book of Revelation) he is seen standing at the birth of a child:

> "... She was in labour, crying aloud with the pangs of childbirth. ... the dragon stopped in front of the woman who was having the child so that he could eat it as soon as it was born."
>
> *Apocalypse* 12:2-4

in his rôle as accuser before God, he is seen lurking malevolently at the birth. The same point is made in the *Mishnah*.

In the original Creation story, God made some promises, two of them were: that the woman and Satan would be enemies of each other until the woman and her offspring would destroy Satan; and that the woman give birth in pain.

It is interesting to note how often the ideas of birth and evil are associated both in the Scriptures and in myths, this will be explored later.

In the final departure from Egypt, we see Satan in his rôle as Angel of Death. Here God shows his power over him by a strict selection of the victims -

> "put the blood of the lambs on the door posts ... the Lord will not allow the Destroyer to enter your houses".

13

God, we are reassured, has the ultimate power over Satan. Meanwhile, however, he is allowed to

> "roam to and fro on the earth"
>
> Job 1:7

and it is for us to be alert.

The Satan of the Scripture seems to perform three functions; he seduces men, he accuses them before God, and he is the bringer of death.

Each appearance of Satan leaves us with a paradox. Why is a seemingly perfect creation, infected by an evil seductive personification of wickedness? Why does a good God seemingly create this evil being? If Satan was originally created good, how did he become evil? Actually a careful reading of the story reveals the fact that evil existed without the Serpent, the knowledge of good and evil was there already. God himself pointed out the

> "tree of the knowledge of good and evil".
>
> *Genesis* 2:16

it was decidedly part of his creation. But is God himself not heard as saying that

> "He saw everything he had made, and behold it was very good"
>
> *Genesis* 1:31

- a strange paradox. There is obviously more to the story than

14

meets the eye.

The very fact that God is seen as pointing out the tree of the knowledge of good and evil indicates that he intended man to have a choice, that there was always a possibility of good or evil. Man was not created as a pre-programmed robot, but as a free being with choices.

- The Fall - a Point in History -

If we see the story of the Serpent in the Garden as the story of the fall of man, then we see man as having been created perfect and weakened by his experience of the original sin. Man then experiences this cosmic sin, or evil, as the falling short of, or failing to become, what God the creator intends him to be. This cosmic sin is seen as having as its root cause alienation from God, our source of sustenance as human beings.

This cosmic (or original) sin first spoken of in the 'Serpent in the garden of Eden' story has a solution which is both complex and difficult to understand; it can be dealt with only by a restoring of our source of sustenance and we cannot do it for ourselves, with God's help (grace) alone can we become complete and whole people.

The devil and evil could then be seen either as failings or weaknesses within the heart of man, or external forces present in the world to lead us away from God, our source of sustenance on the journey through life. All three functions of Satan could also equally be seen as coming from within man, as the natural outcome of the weakness of the human condition.

Whether we see the Devil in this story as an evil force within the heart of man, or whether we see him as an influence from

15

without, we are certainly warned of the power and wiliness of this personification of wickedness. Both the Jewish Talmud and the Christian Fathers agree on his seductive influence over men.

God, we have been reassured, has the ultimate power over Satan. Meanwhile, however, he is allowed to 'roam to and fro on the earth' [Job 1:7] and it is for us to be alert. Why does God allow such an evil presence to roam the earth? A question hurled at God throughout the history of the world, through both the Hebrew and the Christian eras. How many voices were raised to God from the terror of the Holocaust ''Why O God ...?'' The Talmud seeks to explain that the 'Prompter to evil' is an essential constituent in human nature, a force without which the race would soon be extinct. If the 'Prompter' is seen in terms of drives within the hearts of all men - as anger, lust, power - then we see our need for them.

The question, why does God allow evil, is exposed by the mystic Julian of Norwich, who in her Divine Revelations faced the tension she saw as existing between the Love of God and the existence of Sin. Her courage in confronting God with her dilemma was rewarded by the revelation,

> ''... Sin is behovable (necessary, inevitable), but all shall be well, and all shall be well, and all manner of things shall be well ...''
>
> [Julian of Norwich 'Revelations of Divine Love' Ch. 27]

We had already been reassured that 'all would be well', that God had ultimate power over evil; but that sin should be 'necessary', gives a whole new dimension to the story.

> ''O certe necessarium Adae peccatum, quod Christi

morte deletum est!
O felix culpa, quae talem ac tantum meruit habere Re-
demptorem!"

"O most needful sin of Adam which was blotted out
by the death of Christ!
O happy fault that merited so great a Redeemer!"
[from the Exultet of the Easter Vigil service]

- Cosmic Evil, a different perspective -

Rather than seeing this 'cosmic' or 'original' sin as something
initiated at a certain point in time, it may be that the whole story
of the Garden of Eden can be seen as a representation of a
promise - if man is faithful, the universe will be guided towards
a new state.

Perhaps Creation was not a 'once and for all' act, perhaps
Creation is something that is in the process of becoming. The
God who saw that what he had made was good, had initiated
something dynamic; a system in which matter would eventually
decay as Creation strove towards its eventual goal.

"... the whole earth is groaning in travail ..."
Paul's letter to the Romans 8:22

The God-given tension that exists in Creation between Involution
or entropy (the natural tendency of matter to decay, and chaos)
on the one hand, and the Evolution towards Spirit (the striving
to bring about the New Creation) on the other, is dramatised in
the story of Adam and Eve in the Garden.

17

The Original Sin expresses and personifies, in one localised act, the perennial and universal law of imperfection which operates in mankind by virtue of its being 'in the process of becoming'. Man and Creation are striving towards their ultimate goal.

In the material world, physical disorder of one sort or another must necessarily be produced spontaneously in a system which is developing its organic character, so long as the system is incompletely organised. Original Sin is the symbolism of the inevitable chance of evil that exists when finite beings strive to achieve progress.

From this point of view, the Garden of Eden story is no longer the story of a mistake at a point in history. Evil is no longer an unforseen accident in the universe. It is an 'enemy' inevitably produced by God, simply by the fact that He decided on creation - new forces and new matter brought into being unrefined are dangerous things full of potential but also of pain.

In a sense, evil is a natural spin-off from the birth of such potential. This theory may illuminate the truths hidden in the myths connecting evil with birth. It throws new light on the stories of Satan, when he is seen acting in the rôle of the Accuser at the birth of a child.

The God-given goal and the apex of this struggle is the Second Coming, the New Creation, the Coming of the Messiah. God, the Alpha and the Omega, the beginning and the end. The placing of the coming of the Messiah at the apex and at the axis of a growing Creation in no way contradicts the Christian view that the Messiah emerged for a short time into the field of human experience about two thousand years ago. In a point in time he is seen on the Cross - the very real personification of the struggle against the very evil inherent in the Creation he himself knew he was the axis and the apex of -

"'I am the Alpha and the Omega', the beginning and the end".

Revelation 21:6

The triumph of the Resurrection story is a foreshadowing of the eventual triumph of good over evil, of life over death, of the Messiah coming in glory, of the final result of the struggle - the new Creation. It should give confidence to those who acknowledge the inherent risk of imperfection in our world and in ourselves.

"O see, in guilt I was born
a sinner was I conceived"

Psalm 50[51]:5

There seems to be an in-built knowledge of this sin into which we are born, or even conceived. This knowledge has lead to a whole theology of the need for Purification, for Protection, for Expiation, for Redemption. Throughout societies, the Rites and Rituals surrounding the celebration of a new-born child contain some element of this calling on the Almighty to protect the child; some sort of purification ritual is also found.

The religious service of 'Churching of Women' still found in some Christian traditions appears to have been borrowed from the Mosaic law (Leviticus 12:6) which is concerned with the purification of the woman after childbirth, and the presentation of the child to God (Luke 2:22); though those services in actual use in the Western Christian Church are of medieval date and emphasise thanksgiving for safe recovery from childbirth and for the safe delivery of the child, rather than the purification of the woman and the presentation of a sin offering. Interestingly, even in its sanitised form, the service usually includes a reference to cleanliness and purity:

> "Who shall climb the mountain of the Lord?
> Who shall stand in his holy place?
> The man with clean hands and pure heart,
> ..."

Psalm 23[24] verses 3 & 4

With our more positive view of evil, we could also see these initiation rites as preparation for the battle ahead; the Almighty the Source of sustenance (grace) is acknowledged.

In the struggle of creation towards the Second Coming, towards its apex, the Omega point, we break free from the bondage of sin by the Grace of God. Grace is our sustenance, God the Alpha and the Omega of his evolving Creation, is its source. Alienation from the Eternal Source results in a lack of the sustenance needed to continue the struggle; a cessation of the struggle results in bondage to sin.

The two prayers for deliverance from evil, quoted earlier:

> "May it be thy will, O Lord my God and God of my fathers, to deliver me this day and every day from shamelessness and shameless men, from an evil man, an evil companion and an evil neighbour, and from an evil occurrence: from the corrupting tempter, and from an unjust judgement and an unjust opponent, be he a son of the covenant or be he not a son of the covenant."

> "Our Father in Heaven, hallowed be your name. Your

kingdom come, your will be done on earth as it is in Heaven. Give us this day our daily bread and forgive us our trespasses as we forgive them who trespass against us. And cause us not to be lead into temptation, but deliver us from evil''

are human responses to our contact with evil and sin and give us some idea of the usual way in which we see sin in everyday life. They show that deep in our being we are aware that, on our own, without God, we are unable to overcome or break free from evil.

- Sin -

We need to remember that evil is not always what we do as individuals but also what has been done to us, there is innocent suffering. Our response to what has been done to us is important - it can either trap us into personal sin or free us; we as individuals have a responsibility for it as it applies to us personally - our particular sins. Sin, in general, is universal but often covered up, only God can deal with it; only God can reveal its true nature to us.

When not dealt with, sin leads to other things, such as sickness and loneliness, war, crime and injustice. If the various means of dealing with this do not get to the roots, then more sickness and loneliness are created. Forgiveness is an important factor in its resolution, but even forgiveness depends upon the grace of God. An acknowledgement of our state of sinfulness and of our need for forgiveness can be found in the annual Jewish liturgy of Atonement (*Yom Kippur*), and in the Christian sacrament of penance.

- Confession of Sin brings us in touch with reality -

This is what the psalms do for us: they show us it is safe to be open with God and explore those bits of us we are afraid to face. These bits are sinful because; sometimes they represent wilful sinful acts, sometimes sinful responses to what other people's sinful behaviour has done to us, and finally the pain we suffer in innocence because we are all born into a fallen world in which just the fact of living in it (with the activities of Satan) inflicts sin upon us.

This 'infliction' is not often direct from Satan and his spiritual colleagues. Usually it is seen as 'the way things are'. Any observer can see these negative and hurtful aspects of the world, even birth has this in it for many people. Our childhood nurture and the culture of the society into which we happen to be born and were nurtured, feeds us with its prejudices that are often sinful.

Our healing and deliverance from all these things demand that they be in the first place exposed to ourselves, and then, as an act of will on our part, to God. When this is done, then God is able to bring about a healing. We do not come to God after we have cleaned ourselves up in order to be truly acceptable to him. We come as we are, with all our mess, so that he can clean us up and make us acceptable to ourselves because we are always acceptable to him, so constant is his love.

Use of the psalms in an honest way that helps us to become aware of what is in us, speaks to our real condition and assures us that nothing needs to be 'bracketed out' as in some liturgical uses of the psalms. All is human, all is a part of me and all is redeemable by God's Grace. Total response to God involves total giving of ourselves by not hiding anything that is in us.

An inadequate view of sin will lead us to adopt a 'good boy or girl, collector of cub or brownie points' stance, as a response to our sins. This destroys our full humanity and causes mental illnesses like depression, because in seeking to avoid facing those sinful tendencies that are in us, we also deny parts of ourselves that are potentially good and creative. By looking at specific psalms that refer to specific traits, defenses and neurotic behaviour patterns that afflict all kinds of people, I hope to apply in a practical way all that has been said in this chapter.

Finally, the Christian Gospel is Good News because it says 'God so loved that he gave'. This is the authentic Divine voice that crosses all racial, political and religious divides. The voice of man says 'You will be OK if you keep this or that set of rules', but it gives no help or encouragement, it destroys; it is bad news. All God asks is an honest response to his giving of himself. The basic aim therefore of this work is to give something that will help people to make this honest response. Many will be offended because there is something in our nature that finds simple honest responses inadequate or perhaps vulgar. Could it be pride, the worst of all sins? Or just that we feel threatened when our powerlessness in large areas of life is exposed.

CHAPTER 1:2

HUMAN NATURE: INDIVIDUAL RESPONSE TO THE HURTS OF A FALLEN WORLD

As we pass through life from conception to death, the responses we make to what happens to us are complex and not very easy to understand. To complete this life pilgrimage, spiritual growth and self-awareness are needed; for all of us, it would seem, this is a long and painful process of learning, based upon experience combined with honest self-reflection.

Understanding of the heart needs to balance understanding of the intellect so that, working together, they can give us insight into our own nature. Our present approach to education so undervalues this balance, that in only a few exceptional cases do people have the will to enter into this hard and slow discipline which is, in essence, a personal pilgrimage.

As we develop, from the womb onwards, we build defenses, like a protective shield, around us as a means of survival in an imperfect world. When we experience emotions we find too difficult to cope with, we tend to bury them but later have to find indirect ways of handling them. This way of coping, though unavoidable and necessary for our self-preservation, in some way affects the way we see the world and each other; this building of defense mechanisms, thus, has both a positive and a negative aspect.

The positive aspect of this defense building is that it provides us with a kind of protective shell and prevents our soul from being utterly destroyed in the extremes of pain and hurt of life. It also enables us to live, survive, and cope with relationships with other people.

The negative side to this coping technique is that we can deceive ourselves into believing that our defense mechanisms are really our true selves, and the messages they give us about the world outside ourselves are objectively true. If we withdraw with fear from a relationship with a person because that person makes us feel uncomfortable, we assume that this other person must be at fault (that they are either horrible, wicked or mad) because of the way our defense mechanism distorts what is objectively true. We could well be very wrong about them. The problem could lie entirely within a hurt part of our own soul, the person with whom we feel uncomfortable could well be more whole than we are. Our defense mechanisms can, in many cases, distort our perception of others.

This same coping technique, instead of distorting someone's perception of others, can equally, for some people, distort their perception of themselves. In the same situation, these people think they are totally at fault and that the other person is perfectly OK. Their defense mechanism has given them the reverse message: that the objective world 'out there' is good and they are bad. Some go from this point to really believe that they must be the cause of the bad things that happen in the world.

To get a more objectively true view of life, an understanding of defense mechanisms and how they work is essential. Whether we habitually deny those emotions we find difficult to cope with (and become depressed), or whether we habitually project our unacceptable emotions onto other people (and become paranoid), we need to understand our own defenses and be able to see the real person who is behind them and larger than them. When we are willing to do this, we can recognise defenses in others, increase our own understanding of them, and be able to forgive them.

Many of the psalms express aspects of these defense mechanisms; the lines of quiet despair, phrases of naked rage, are only two of the very real emotions expressed in the psalms. These uncovered emotional outbursts sometimes strike us as appalling; nevertheless, if they are our own defense mechanisms that are being expressed we will feel in sympathy with them. If we do not recognise our own emotions in them, we will tend to react against them. God knows our need to express our feelings openly to him so that we can let him in behind them and he can then help us to ...

"know as fully as I am known"

1 *Cor.* 13:12 [JB]

which is where our spiritual pilgrimage should be leading us. There is a saying "to know all is to forgive all", we are often unable to forgive, both others and ourselves, because we do not understand our defense mechanisms and as a result cannot meet the real person who lives behind them.

There are a number of approaches to understanding our defense mechanisms, but I am using those described in Frank Lake's book *Clinical Theology*. When I have described the particular defense mechanisms, I will quote some relevant passages from the psalms to illustrate how they work themselves through within individual human experience. But before doing this, two more points need to be made:

i - The defense mechanisms are not sin in themselves but are the result of primal sin. They happen because of our human frailty which, in turn, is a result of being born into a sinful or fallen world - a world in which nothing is complete or perfect; as a result of this, many people have become alienated from the love of God, the ultimate source of healing and wholeness.

"O see in guilt I was born
a sinner was I conceived"

Psalm 51(50):5

Of course, this psalm is not saying that sex, conception and birth are wicked acts in themselves; but that the world into which we are conceived is imperfect, and is able to have sinful or bad effects upon us from conception onwards.

If we recognise our defense mechanisms as: 'the tools we have become in the habit of using, in our attempts to survive the sinful effects of an imperfect world', then we will be motivated to seek God's grace to cope with them positively. If not, we will be led into acts of sin, simply by acting upon the distorted messages our defense mechanisms convey to us.

ii - When we are able to operate our defense mechanisms then we cope with life and are able to survive. We can operate them either in a positive and creative way, or as we sometimes do, in a negative and destructive way (neurotic behaviour). In extreme cases where the ability to operate defense mechanisms breaks down, then people 'go to pieces' or have a breakdown (psychotic behaviour).

It shows how we need these defense mechanisms for survival in this world because nobody can afford to expose their naked soul, except to particularly loving and understanding people. In the end only God can know all, love all and accept all that we are. I think the psalms are vehicles by which this 'love of God' can be experienced, and positive defenses for coping with this world built up. My experience of prayer using the psalms is one in which all defensive inhibitions go down until prayer is ended, then they can be taken up again for the time being so that I can cope with relationships in this world. As we look in more detail at these defense mechanisms, what has just been stated in outline will be developed more specifically.

For the person concerned with day to day living, it is obvious that the positive, creative way of operating defense mechanisms needs to be employed. While still living in this world we need them, but if we adopt the negative, destructive way of just being neurotic and saying 'that is the way I am', we will do so only at great expense to those people with whom we have to live. Indeed, many people do this because of their spiritual immaturity and unwillingness to face themselves. If such people are clever, strong willed or dominant in any way, they can create groups around themselves; religious sects, movements or political parties that are just an extension of their own neuroses. There are also many cases of such people creating a neurotic family in the same way.

In all these cases of people who seem to be 'on top' and coping well by being neurotic, a common feature is lack of awareness. They usually believe that they are OK and all others are wrong. The self deception has a strong spiritual dimension. In scripture, Satan is the deceiver. Alienation from God gives the power for the deceit to operate, whereas openness to God gives release from this power, but it also brings the pain that goes with knowing the truth. The basis of this is our own vulnerability. We cannot afford to be too vulnerable in this present world because we will be walked all over; but paradoxically, we need to be open and vulnerable in order to be released from the dominance of our defense mechanisms and healed of our neuroses.

I think this fact of our existence explains all the paradoxes we find in scripture and especially so in the life of Christ. It is a seemingly weak crucified Christ who saves us, not a powerful conquering hero of the kind that the neurotic world admires and understands.

This paradox runs right through the psalms; they seem to have a dual purpose. In their words we see two conflicting messages: one is, God speaking to us; and the other is, like a mirror, showing us what we are like. These defense mechanisms about which so much has been said are all reflected in this second aspect of the psalms.

In this work, you are invited to look at both of these aspects. To see your own defense mechanisms mirrored, and also to see the love of God revealed. When you recognise both of these things you can then, in your quiet times with God, learn how to drop the defenses and expose your soul naked towards the God who can give you strength. This can start a process whose end could be that defense mechanisms are no longer required and we see ourselves, God and others as they really are.

> "For our knowledge is imperfect ...
> ... but when the perfect comes, the imperfect will pass away. ...
> ... For now we see in a mirror dimly, but then face to face. Now I know in part; then I shall understand fully, even as I have been fully understood."
>
> 1 *Corinthians* 13:9

In the following chapters, five types of defense mechanisms will be examined and at the end of each one, one or two psalms relevant to that particular defense will be given.

CHAPTER 2:1

DEFENSE MECHANISMS:
DEPRESSIVE PERSONALITY

The depressive type defense mechanism is basically a defense that 'bottles up' and denies all those feelings that are thought to be bad and unacceptable. This 'bottling up' process becomes so habitual that it takes place without the person realising it and causes those who operate in this way to become joyless, solid, heavy like lead, or even to feel dead inside. It takes time to reach a severe state of depression but the process begins very early and slowly gets a grip on a person.

The reason why people adopt this method of defense against the world's hurts is twofold:

One factor is the nature of the person. This tends to be predominantly one of 'flight' from, or avoidance of, those unpleasant emotions that make a person feel uncomfortable; this is combined with a high degree of introversion. In all of us there is a need to feel accepted, especially a need to feel accepted by those important to us for our wellbeing, such as parents. People with an avoidance type nature feel that they might be rejected if they have anything in them that is likely to offend the parent (or other significant person). These 'wicked' things are then hidden and denied and what is called by some 'a compulsive compliant' personality is developed.

The other factor is the kind of parent (or other adult) they experience in early life. If these adults demand of the infant and developing child, standards of behaviour which are found too hard to live up to, then, in the first instance, within them rage, protest and other unacceptable feelings begin to well up. This is then met with a strong 'contra' reaction of either 'Mummy won't love you' or 'Daddy won't accept a child who behaves like this'. In response to this, it is not long before the infant learns to bottle up these strongly reactive feelings against excessive demands, and works hard to meet them. From this early experience, a defense mechanism is built up which is then continued throughout adult life as a habitual behaviour pattern; this, in the end, destroys the soul's inner peace.

Let us now develop this further:

In adult relationships, because of the fear of rejection, such people never say what they really feel and are always trying hard to please others. As a result, they use up too much energy and are quickly exhausted. It is at this point that depression sets in; it feels like a black cloud covering them.

At work, these people never complain but work harder and harder until they collapse. They are very moral people, given to feeling guilty over trivial things. In their spiritual life, they seek perfection and desire to be inscrutable models of faith. It is easy to see why such people have strong suicidal tendencies to which they will never admit, because such feelings are contrary to faith. These tendencies towards suicide come about because their anger is so bottled up that it can only be turned inward against their worthless selves. God is a larger than life projection of their over demanding parent and is therefore to be feared and appeased by putting on a good show of goodness. Sadly underneath this 'good show' is a terrible fear of judgement. The love of God is simply not understood and forgiveness does not seem possible for such a wretch.

The FAULT lies in two things for this kind of person, and both originate in childhood nurture:

The first cause is that other people, and especially authority figures, are harsh, demanding, unloving and unforgiving; expecting purity, perfection and all other virtues; but judging heavily all forms of weakness.

The second one is a belief that the only way to survive is to hide all these weaker and 'bad' things from them. All will then be well. The torment is that this does not work.

This twofold belief is then projected onto God making the whole of creation appear a living hell in the experience of such a person.

The CURE is simply to help the depressive (the 'bottler up') to see that the world is not like this. God is not a projection of over demanding parents and adult authority figures. Our starting point is aptly expressed in the following words of Isaiah:

"Let the wicked man abandon his way,
the evil man his thoughts.
Let him turn back to Yahweh who will take pity on him,
to our God who is rich in forgiving;
for my thoughts are not your thoughts,
my ways not your ways - it is Yahweh who speaks.
Yes, the heavens are as high above the earth
as my ways are above your ways,
my thoughts above your thoughts."

Isaiah 55:7,8,9 [Jerusalem Bible]

The following two psalms are key ones in understanding the depressive's problem, and dealing with it.

They are firstly *Psalms* 31(32)

"I kept it secret and my frame was wasted.
I groaned all the day long
for night and day your hand
was heavy upon me.
Indeed, my strength was dried up
as by the summer's heat"

Ps 31(32):3,4

It shows the depressive's history of bottling up feelings, and describes well the negative effect it has on such a person. This theme is repeated in many other psalms. The feelings are of sin and guilt, bad things that God does not like. The answer to this problem comes when that which is 'bottled up' is let out.

"But now I have acknowledged my sins;
my guilt I did not hide.
I said 'I will confess
my offence to the Lord'.
And you Lord, have forgiven
the guilt of my sin."

Ps 31(32):5

This then leads to relief, God does not condemn but forgives

"So let every good man pray to you
in time of need.
The floods of water may reach high
but him they shall not reach.
You are my hiding place, O Lord;
you save me from distress.
(You surround me with cries of deliverance.)"

The sufferer is then restored and therefore, in this formal liturgical setting, we get the statement of truth about God's nature at the beginning. In real life experience, this discovery comes last.

> "Happy the man whose offence is forgiven,
> whose sin is remitted.
> O happy the man to whom the Lord
> imputes no guilt,
> in whose spirit is no guile."

Ps 31(32):1,2

Secondly, *Psalm* 57(58).
This psalm is therapeutic for the depressive. It shows that negative, violent and strongly destructive emotions can safely be poured out to God. Whereas other people cannot always cope with them, God can, and for emotional and spiritual health they must be given to him.

The psalm begins with honest questions that each of us, when in distress, really need to ask God, but often feel we dare not.

> "Do you truly speak justice, you who hold divine power?
> Do you mete out fair judgement to the sons of men?"

Ps 57(58):1

Following the asking of this question to God, the emotional flood-gates open, and verses 6-10 pour out vindictive spite in raw emotional form.

"O God, break the teeth in their mouths,
tear out the fangs of these wild beasts, O Lord!
Let them vanish like water that runs away:
let them wither like grass that is trodden underfoot:
let them be like the snail that dissolves into slime:
like a woman's miscarriage that never sees the sun."

Ps 57(58):6-8

This outpouring needs to occur to drain the spiritual puss from the boil caused by the unjust hurts inflicted so often on many people who live in this fallen world. Those who feel free to do this, because they have learned to believe in God's mercy, end up with a faith that in the end God will put things right.

"'Truly,' men shall say, 'the just are rewarded.
Truly, there is a God who does justice on earth'"

Ps 57(58):11

I often encourage depressed people to chant this to themselves repeatedly to help them get in touch with those emotions they bottle up because they find them hard to free. Religious communities need to use this psalm regularly in their liturgies and to identify with the feelings in it. There is often someone who 'gets up our nose', whose teeth we would love to 'break in their mouths'; chanting such a psalm can help clear up this emotion before God, free us, and help us truly to love and accept such people. To bottle it up can cause that depressed heavy feeling to hang over a community.

When Jesus Christ hung on the cross, many people railed on him and poured their spite out. Mark tells us:

"... those who passed by derided him, wagging their heads, and saying 'Aha! You who would destroy the temple and build it in three days, save yourself, and come down from the cross!' So also the chief priests mocked him to one another with the scribes, saying, 'He saved others; he cannot save himself. Let the Christ, the King of Israel, come down now from the cross, that we may see and believe.' Those who were crucified with him also reviled him."

Mark 15:29-32

Christians see this as a fulfilment of the messianic prophecy in Isaiah chapter 53.

Frank Lake in *Clinical Theology* says:

"Should he fail to take account of God's work in Christ, a man may well affirm that all things work together for evil, as if calculated to drive him to despair. The same man, bearing in mind the resources that are available in the loving, recreative, personal relationships offered by God and man, will come eventually to know that 'all things work together for good to them that love God'. There is no human experience which cannot be put on to the anvil of a lively relationship with God and man, and battered into a meaningful shape."

Clinical Theology, Frank Lake, DLT 1966 p. 97

This last sentence, in particular, is one we all need to bear in mind in relation to our despairing and depressed moments.

CHAPTER 2:2

DEFENSE MECHANISMS: ANXIETY STATES

The term 'anxiety states' covers a wide variety of ways in which people experience the type of anxiety that could be seen as being abnormal. Anxiety itself is an emotion that is essential for a healthy existence; it warns of danger and stimulates actions that are creative. Without healthy anxiety, we could not live a full life, and when danger threatens it is essential for our survival.

Abnormal anxiety is anxiety which is either present in excessive amounts, or related to experiences that are not in reality threatening. Sometimes, in over-anxious people, fears or worries seem to be created in the imagination; and at other times the anxiety seems to be projected onto situations (or other people) out of all proportion to the threat they present.

The problem such people have is that their anxiety is out of control. It drives them into all kinds of odd behaviour, or floods over them like an uncontrollable fog. It rises up within them, making them twitchy, knotting the guts, causing blood pressure to be raised, quickening the breathing and making the whole self feel as if it is disintegrating. The anxious person lives on a knife edge, in permanent fear of 'going to pieces' or being 'sucked into a black hole'.

They are difficult for others to live with because they create a restless atmosphere, they are pernickety, agitated and never at peace; anxiety states appear to be 'catching', in the first place anxious people 'caught' it from mother, or at some other point in their early nurture. Such people are always very sensitive by nature and this may well be one of the reasons that they become vulnerable to having excessive amounts of anxiety in the first place.

The cause of anxiety states

It is true to say that all anxiety states are caused by having to live in an imperfect world, the effects of which threaten an individual's sense of inner security. For many, the anxiety state originates in the womb where feelings are, in some sense, transmitted through the umbilical cord from mother to child. In people whose first experience of anxiety came this way, two features of anxiety are common:

The first one is a feeling of knotting of the guts, sometimes so severe that it is almost unbearable. Any anxiety-raising situation will cause this, but sometimes it happens for no apparent reason.

The second one is a feeling of not being secure, so continually present that the afflicted person has to look for something to worry about. In essence, their anxiety is 'free floating' in that it is not attached to anything objective happening in the present moment. There are people of whom it is often said that they spend their lives looking for something to worry about.

There are however many people who do not experience anxiety in this way, but who are equally crippled by it. These are the ones who tend to live in a continuous fog of anxiety that touches them all over, moving from one part of the body to another; sometimes focusing itself in the neck, back, arms, chest or almost anywhere; in headaches, palpitations, breathlessness, or in the bizarre sensation of feeling as if the blood is like fizzy pop.

How such people attempt to deal with their anxiety

There seems to be three main ways in which people attempt to deal with their anxiety; all of these ways work only partially and all of them also create more problems:

-i- Projection

This method of dealing with anxiety is very common and involves placing the anxiety onto some other object, person or situation.

Anxious people often have a wide variety of phobias that are objectively irrational, such as a fear of spiders, feathers etc. It is surprising how many people, who would in all other ways appear to be very balanced, have such phobias. Those suffering from anxiety states do have phobias that are severe and disabling at times, making their lives a misery. Many people have phobias that are only a focus for anxiety; as such, they are useful and are not a serious problem.

When the anxious person projects their anxiety onto other people, then they become very difficult to live with. They expect all of their friends to share their anxieties in full and even believe that their fears are universal and objectively valid. This often makes honest sharing with them difficult. Whenever an anxious person is around, everyone who is in the least bit sensitive tenses up.

-ii- Adopting a rigidly obsessive life style

People who adopt a rigidly obsessive life style are said by some to have an 'obsessional personality'. The rigidly obsessional behaviour is an attempt by the sufferer to control the anxiety. Common obsessions are often to do with cleanliness or security. Cleanliness involves constant hand washing, sterilising of all

41

utensils, and house pride which involves hours of dusting and polishing. Security expresses itself in checking and double checking everything and making sure one always gets things right. Rigid religious observation can also be an aspect of this. These habits can be virtues if kept in balance, but the anxious person goes over the top with them, sensing danger where no danger exists. It is quite easy to understand that the source of all human anxiety is to do with feeling insecure in a sometimes very threatening world, but for anxiety to work for our benefit it must be proportional to the objective content of the threat. It is therefore a matter of degree that is not always easy to recognise. What is obsessional to one person is common sense precaution to another, and what appears to be careless indifference to one can be plain common sense to another. It would seem that it all depends upon the level of our anxiety as an individual, and what experiences activate it, as to whether we see behaviour as being obsessive or not.

-iii- Repression and Denial

Repression and denial are largely unconscious ways of dealing with anxiety, a person is not usually aware that they are doing it. When anxiety is successfully repressed and denied, a person forms a habitual lifestyle in which no anxiety, or at least very little, is actually felt. This in turn causes other problems. The major problem, experienced by this type of person, is depression ('bottling it all up'). Many counsellors experience the problem of an anxious person who has 'bottled it all up' successfully, and thereby become depressed; when helped to overcome their depression, they become persons with an anxiety state. The anxiety that has been locked away for years suddenly flows out all over the place, rendering the sufferer powerless; they then tend to complain endlessly later. In most cases, people say that they would rather be depressed than anxious, just like the Children of Israel complained to Moses after the Exodus that they would rather return to bondage in Egypt than suffer the anxiety of being free in the wilderness.

> "Why did we not die at Yahweh's hand in the land of Egypt, when we were able to sit down to pans of meat and could eat bread to our heart's content! As it is, you have brought us to this wilderness to starve this whole company to death!"
>
> (*Exodus* 16:3 *Jerusalem Bible*)

Nevertheless, the change from depression to anxiety is progress in spiritual and emotional terms. Therefore the correct agenda is to move on towards coming to terms with and controlling the anxiety; because properly managed, anxiety can be a creative means for bringing about change and growth.

The other main way in which the repression and denial of anxiety takes place is to convert it into paranoia. As this will be examined in detail next, there is no need to say more about it here. It is also true to say that hysterical and schizoid personality problems have within them an anxiety element, because anxiety is always part of the human beings' emotional make-up. What therefore has been said here can at times apply to them, indeed, everyone has to deal with their inner anxiety at some time or other, in one way or another. I will therefore conclude with an examination of Psalm 45(46) which is a standard 'anxiety' one, suitable for all anxious people at all times.

> "God is for us a refuge and strength,

a helper close at hand in time of distress;
so we should not fear though the earth should rock,
though the mountains fall into the depths of the sea
even though its waters rage and foam,
even though the mountains be shaken by its waves.''

"The Lord of hosts is with us;
the God of Jacob is our stronghold"

Psalm 45(46):1-3 & 7

It adequately describes how such people feel, and contrasts this with God's power. It is when one is able to trust realistically in God's boundless power, despite what is happening in the world around, that anxiety is kept within bounds. Hence the statement in the first verse:

"God is for us a refuge and strength,
a helper close at hand in time of distress;"

Psalm 45(46):1

Verses 2 and 3 go on to show how the anxious person feels, namely that the whole world is crumbling around them; but ends with the affirmation that God is in control.

"so we should not fear though the earth should rock,
though the mountains fall into the depths of the sea
even though its waters rage and foam,
even though the mountains be shaken by its waves.
The Lord of hosts is with us:
the God of Jacob is our stronghold."

Psalm 45(46):2 & 3

The rest of the psalm repeats this theme.

I often get anxious people to sit still in an upright position after reading the whole psalm and repeat the first line of verse 11:

> "Be still and know that I am God"
>
> *Psalm* 45(46):10

Breathing deeply in and out with the rhythm of the words. I have found this to be a successful way of lowering anxiety in most people. To begin with I do it with them until they are confident that they know what to do, and then I encourage them to make it a regular practice not only when they are in a state of acute anxiety, but for about twenty minutes every day. It is a good basis from which other meditative prayer exercises can be developed. Psalms 123(124), 124(125) and 129(130) are also good psalms for anxious people to meditate upon.

High levels of anxiety in people are directly related to low levels of trust in God; or lack of confidence in the trustworthiness of some being who has ultimate control of the world in which we live, and who is able to bring about a good end to whatever it is that we find threatening at any specific time in our lives. Excessive anxiety is almost equal to faithlessness. In the gospels, Jesus frequently makes this connection and on many occasions tells the disciples not to be afraid. He seeks to encourage an attitude of trust that would cure anxiety. Perhaps one of the most striking passages that illustrates this is a passage from the gospel according to Matthew:

> "Therefore I tell you, do not be anxious about your life, what you shall eat or what you shall drink, nor about your body, what you shall put on. Is not life

more than food, and the body more than clothing? Look at the birds of the air; they neither sow nor reap nor gather into barns, and yet your heavenly Father feeds them. Are you not of more value than they? And which of you by being anxious can add one cubit to his span of life? And why are you anxious about clothing? Consider the lilies of the field, how they grow; they neither toil nor spin; yet I tell you even Solomon in all his glory was not arrayed like one of these. But if God so clothes the grass of the field, which today is alive and tomorrow is thrown into the oven, will he not much more clothe you, O men of little faith? Therefore do not be anxious, saying, 'What shall we eat?' or 'What shall we drink' or 'What shall we wear?' For the Gentiles seek all these things; and your heavenly Father knows that you need them all. But seek first his kingdom and his righteousness, and all these things shall be yours as well."

Matthew 6:25-34

This sermon is worth learning by heart and meditating upon, as is also a passage from Paul's letter to the Philippians:

"Rejoice in the Lord always; again I will say, Rejoice. Let all men know your forbearance. The Lord is at hand. Have no anxiety about anything, but in everything by prayer and supplication with thanksgiving let your requests be made known to God. And the peace of God, which passes all understanding, will keep your hearts and your minds in Christ Jesus."

Philippians 4:4-7

Anyone who has been engaged in counselling people suffering from excessive anxiety, or seeking to help them in any way will be aware of how difficult this problem is at a human level.

There are many therapies and anxiety management techniques which are applied at a purely secular level, and do help to some degree, but often leave the hard core of anxiety in some people untouched. It seems to me that a supernatural 'touch of God' is required for many to be healed. This is because anxiety in many cases is a result of alienation from God, which in turn is a result of sin. Not sin committed by the anxious individual, but sin done against or inflicted upon them by circumstances well out-side their control at a time of high vulnerability in their lives.

There are also many 'religious' attitudes which cause further anxiety and are inflicted on people in the name of God by people who work to a religious system of doctrine at a superfi-cial intellectual level, but themselves do not trust God or have a practical living faith in him. From this standpoint such people tell the anxious person that if only they could discover a specific sin they have committed and confess it then their anxiety would be taken away. This puts the onus on them in such a way that it makes them worse. It is putting a burden on them too hard to bear. The same thing that Jesus accused the Pharisees of doing.

> "... They bind heavy burdens, hard to bear, and lay them on men's shoulders; but they themselves will not move them with their finger ..."
>
> *Matthew* 23:1-7
> (see also *Luke* 11:37-46)

Therefore, when we see excessive anxiety as a result of sin, we must also see its cure, not in a moral legalistic sense that leads only to further condemnation, but as lying within an act of loving acceptance towards the individual sufferer that can bridge the gap of alienation from God and restore trust. Other human beings can help to bring this about by the quality of their loving acceptance, but the complete deliverance can come only from God.

CHAPTER 2:3

DEFENSE MECHANISMS: PARANOIA

This condition grips everyone from time to time, but there are some for whom it becomes a fixed way of life. It is a feeling that other people are 'getting at us' which makes the affected person become defensive, aggressive, unyielding and therefore impossible to reason with. The main problem about paranoid feelings is that one can never be sure if 'they are getting at me' or if it is in the imagination, just a misinterpretation of what other people's motives are towards us.

There are many people who are not basically paranoid at all, but who can feel so when in threatening situations. These people will always retain the ability to be self-reflective, something which people who are gripped by basic paranoia which has become an entrenched aspect of their lifestyle cannot be. It is these people who will ask the question above, i.e. 'are they really getting at me or is it my imagination?' and not the person who is firmly fixed in the paranoid defense mode.

The cause of paranoia is inner weakness, as well as anxiety, which dare not be admitted for fear that to do so would put the individual so afflicted in such a position of weakness that it would be exploited by others. This exploitation would lead to his or her downfall and even possible destruction. For this reason a person who is in such a state can never be wrong, can never really relax or enjoy intimate relationships. The 'enemy' lurks everywhere and must be watched carefully.

Those who are apparently permanently fixed in paranoid attitudes which permeate their whole lifestyle are very difficult to relate to positively because they genuinely feel that they are right and everyone else is wrong. Dr. Frank Lake (see *Clinical Theology* chapter II and chapter VII in the abridged version) sees this as stemming from severe deprivation of sustenance, both physical and emotional, in infancy. This created such a high level of anxiety about survival as an individual human being that it seems to be indelibly written upon their personalities for life. Such people would not even recognise their need to meditate on psalms that express paranoia, or even see what I am now saying as having any validity for them, or indeed any validity at all, such is the nature of severe paranoia. The fear of admitting any weakness within oneself is so tremendous that the possibility of doing so is wiped out entirely by repression and denial. The means by which this repression and denial is maintained is by the projection on to others of the unacceptable and bad feelings. This gives the impression to others of being a strong definite 'no nonsense about me' person whose main fault is lack of humour and imagination.

What I have just said about paranoia will be appreciated and recognised by those who have to live and work with such people and also by those who are aware that from time to time and in certain situations they have paranoid feelings themselves. Paranoia is catching, everyone who has to live or work with a paranoid person will be aware that they can only cope with them by being paranoid themselves. In their more detached and reflective moments, such people would find it valuable to meditate on some of the 'paranoid' psalms as a means of coping and retaining their own integrity.

Paranoid feelings that come over most people from time to time are also well expressed in the psalms. Threats to security, our wellbeing, stability, changes in our circumstances, being misunderstood, overpowered or cheated; all raise paranoid feelings in us which we need to recognise and deal with positively. If we try to ignore them or push them away, they have a tendency to build up inside us so that they become a permanent part of our attitude to others. In time this will sour us and could even push us into a fixed state of paranoia. To use relevant psalms as a vehicle for letting God take such feelings and thereby opening ourselves to his grace is our wisest course of action in such circumstances. Psalm 40(41) is a good example of a psalm expressing paranoid feelings.

Verses 1-4 express the ideal - the good person whom God will bless for his goodness. All people with paranoid tendencies have a very strong moral sense and look for justice, but they do so without love or humour, and because of this find it impossible to forgive or forget.

> "Happy the man who considers the poor and the weak.
> The Lord will save him in the day of evil,
> will guard him, give him life, make him happy in the land"

> *Psalm* 40(41):1&2

Verses 5-9 express pure paranoid feeling of being 'got at'. Everyone is wishing the worst on the sufferer. In weakness he or she can be trodden under or wiped out. The intimate relationship is one to be feared because in it weakness is exposed and this gives a certain opportunity to others to destroy. Enemies and friends are equal threats in weakness. One can only hold relationships with other people from a position of strength. All words are empty, meaningless and of no support.

51

"My foes are speaking evil against me.
'How long before he dies and his name be forgotten?'
They come to visit me and speak empty words,
their hearts full of malice, they spread it abroad.

My enemies whisper together against me.
They all weigh up the evil which is on me:
'Some deadly thing has fastened upon him,
he will not rise again from where he lies'
Thus even my friend in whom I trusted,
who ate my bread, has turned against me."

Psalm 40(41):5-9

Verses 11-13 show how God alone is seen as being a trustworthy means of help, but he is not seen clearly, only through paranoid eyes -

"Let me rise once more and I will repay them.
By this I shall know that you are my friend,
if my foes do not shout in triumph over me"

Psalm 40(41):11&12

This underlines the need to relate from a position of strength.

I have pointed out that in this case the person who is overwhelmed by paranoid feelings sees God through paranoid eyes, but it is also true that we all see God from where we are now on our life's journey. This is an inevitable fact of which we must always be aware. We should not however be ashamed to express feelings about God and towards him that are distorted because in his infinite love for us as very finite beings he understands and accepts. What we express to God needs to be truthful from the situation in which we now are, but we must never make it into unchanging dogma. As we grow and work through our pain, we change and see things very differently, hence the ending of this psalm with a more objectively real statement about God:

> "Blessed be the Lord, the God of Israel
> from age to age. Amen. Amen."

Psalm 40(41):13

Other psalms which could be used are Psalms 63(64) and 93(94).

CHAPTER 2:4

DEFENSE MECHANISMS: THE SCHIZOID DEFENSE

The word 'Schizoid' is derived from the Greek verb *'schizo'* meaning 'to split'. People who use this form of defense mechanism are those who are able to split off from consciousness their emotional pain, so that it does not hurt or disturb them. They also develop a very good switch-off approach to issues in their everyday lives that can touch off their emotions in a very painful way and give the appearance to others of being cold, indifferent, calm and rational people. They are loners who do not function well in crowds or the public eye and find commitment in personal relationships very difficult. The schizoid is forever struggling to find a vantage point above and outside the pain of being; such people often identify with Job, their Scriptural representative.

Job who felt forgotten by God; his experience: the ultimate horror, dereliction by the source-person. On first reading, the story tells of a good and upright man, a man who had acquired family and wealth; and almost overnight lost the lot - cattle and camels, fields and property, servants and children. But a closer reading shows that Job's affliction did not begin with his sudden loss of family and wealth, he seemed to have a foretaste of his tragedy and pain all his life. When tragedy overtakes him, he does not react with surprise and is not affronted that such a thing should happen to him; he says

> "for the thing that I fear comes upon me,
> and what I dread befalls me."

He does not curse the tragedy nor the instigator of the loss, but instead curses his own conception and birth

> "Let the day perish wherein I was born,
> and the night which said,
> 'A man-child is conceived'"

and continues to curse his nurture and very existence

> "Why was I not as a hidden untimely birth,
> as infants that never see the light"

This deep desire for death and even non existence is the authentic mark of the depths of the schizoid state.

Colin Wilson, in his book, *The Outsider* (V. Gollanz 1956) gives a wonderful description of the schizoid personality defense. He shows how in such people three fears are present: fear of a loss of control of one's own personal world, the closeness of emotional pain to the surface, and despair about one's own personal identity in relationship to others.

Those who employ the schizoid defense do so for fear of being hurt, overwhelmed and destroyed by other people. They do have very strong feelings of anger but they put this into 'deep freeze' to control it. They are angry because they feel nobody can be trusted, especially when they are vulnerable. They are full of despair because nobody, they believe, really cares about them or understands. They also despair because deep down they feel unreal and dread nothingness. The response to this is to go into themselves and become their own philosophers in an attempt to build a meaningful life that is not too dependant on other people. This last point is their strength because if it is successfully pursued they can become 'happy schizoids' and I have come across quite a number of such people in my counselling experience. Those who do not manage to create for themselves a meaningful lifestyle end up in a very bad and negative state as drop-outs, permanently mentally ill, or in a number of cases, commit suicide.

Having done a thumb-nail sketch of the schizoid defense mechanism, which I hope is sufficient to enable readers to recognise any such traits within themselves, I would like to elaborate a few salient points before turning to relevant psalms for meditation.

Why do people adopt the schizoid defense?

It is impossible to say with certainty, but there are two factors which seem to be present in most people of this kind.

The first is that of severe emotional deprivation in infancy. Many never bonded with their mothers and therefore always felt separate from them. For example, I know of a number of such people in middle age who were totally unmoved by their mother's death. They saw the event as though it were any other woman dying as on a television screen. The deprivation can be caused by many things, mostly beyond control of the individuals concerned, but ends up in the mind of the schizoid person as one certain message about life: 'Do not trust people, they will let you down in the end'.

The second factor is that of introversion; I use this word in the Jungian sense as being a person who draws energy from within themselves when in a state of exhaustion. Introverts can restore themselves emotionally by being in isolation from others. In fact, they need periods of isolation in order to live a reasonably balanced and happy life. Too much 'people pressure' destroys them. To use the schizoid defense successfully, it is therefore essential to be quite an introvert.

- How do those who adopt this defense become Happy Schizoids?
This I think is a very important issue pastorally. The answer in short is that they do so by building their own 'Ivory Tower', but it has to be one which has durability. An ivory tower that collapses can drive them in the first instance into hysteria, which we will look at in the next chapter, and when this fails, into desperate paranoia. When a schizoid person becomes hysterical it can only be sustained for a short while. The objective of such behaviour is to manipulate circumstances so that the ivory tower in which they once existed happily can either be rebuilt, or a new one erected. If this mode of behaviour fails then paranoia takes over, and grows worse unless or until a suitable ivory tower is either built or found.

The idea of the ivory tower is important. It is simply a place of security in which a schizoid person can exist securely and feel themselves. Large and very well organised institutions do not appeal as being secure because they tend to be dominated by paranoid people, and hysterics to a lesser degree, who cannot be trusted.

The ivory tower is built out of the schizoid's ability to develop an area of expertise which other people need but which demands little in terms of emotional involvement. They then develop this in relative isolation, as 'back room boys', or by running their own 'one person band'. Examples of this are: computer experts, clock repairers, academics, artists, writers, composers, indeed any function that requires a high degree of skill but is not dependent upon being involved with too many people. An ivory tower built in this way is quite safe and tends to be the most common way in which schizoids can become 'happy'.

A less common way of building the tower is to have a deep relationship with another schizoid in which very deep emotion is expressed. Such people are capable of very strong passion within the context of the right relationship if it can be found. They can learn to trust some very select people, which could well be based upon an infantile kind of bonding. On the few occasions this does happen, it can be healing but when such relationships fail the trauma is great.

The final, and most probably by far the most successful way of building the ivory tower is the religious one. This is especially so if within the sanctuary of the ivory tower a real relationship with God is formed that is direct and does not depend on too many religious structures but uses them wisely. Hence the predominance of a more mystical approach in which God is experienced as the ultimate reliable resource person. The following quotations from the prophet Isaiah illustrate this basic schizoid attitude to God:

> "Trust no more in man
> He has but breath in his nostrils
> How much is he worth?"

> *Isaiah* 2:22 (JB)

and

"Put no trust in princes,
in mortal men in whom there is no help.
Take their breath, they return to clay
and their plans that day come to nothing."

Psalm 145(146):3

or

"Let him turn back to Yahweh who will take pity on
him
to our God who is rich in forgiving
for my thoughts are not your thoughts
my ways are not your ways - it is Yahweh who speaks.
Yes, the heavens are as high above the earth
as my ways are above your ways
my thoughts above your thoughts."

Isaiah 55:7-9 (JB)

- Relating to God

For those who adopt the schizoid defense there is a double pain.
That of separation from and that of commitment to another
person. The pain of separation brings the dread of non-existence,
of nothingness. The pain of commitment brings the continuing
fear of being hurt, crushed, destroyed or abandoned by the person
to whom one has become vulnerable by virtue of the commitment.
This pain has to be borne and worked through and it has to be
the pain of commitment because it is only accepting and working
through this pain that will lead to anything positive. The pain of
non-being that comes from separation leads nowhere. It is a
dead end. Therefore, working through commitment pain only
enables one to become a happy schizoid and the most fruitful

commitment is that to God. Many saints and mystics have taken this line and we are left with their writings, most notable: John of the Cross and Teresa of Avila, Simone Weil, Soren Kirkegaard; and in modern times, according to Frank Lake, Pope John Paul II (see his book *With Great Respect*).

There are two reasons which make the risk of commitment to God worth taking. They are:

Firstly, God, by definition, is not a human being, as I have already pointed out in the quotation from Isaiah; and it was another human being who caused the problem in the first place.

Secondly, from a Christian point of view Christ bore this kind of pain on the cross and is today able to enter into the struggle with the sufferer giving spiritual strength and sustenance both through word and sacrament. These 'non-human' means of grace are most acceptable to such people. Perhaps the Gospel of John 1:1-14 presents Christ in a way most acceptable to those of schizoid disposition.

Those who opt not to tackle the pain of commitment in a spiritual religious way, but go for building the kind of ivory tower in which they can live with the pain of separation could be described as the 'unhappy schizoids' whose towers are very vulnerable to the chances and changes of this world. Non-spiritual ivory towers are much more easily demolished than spiritual ones because the roots they have are in transient things.

All those of this disposition are very vulnerable, even the spiritually soundly based ones, because they are a questioning, non-accepting minority who cannot be fitted easily into any institution or society. They morally offend many because they appear amoral. Their comfort is that Christ was a bit this way inclined and this was part of the reason for his crucifixion.

Finally, a psalm for those who recognise something of themselves in what has been said here. It is Psalm 87(88), the prayer in desolation; for the very schizoid, praying this psalm could be the only comprehensible means of grace and contact with God. It expresses three strong strands of deep pain schizoid people feel:

- i   The pain of separation, all people, including God, who can give comfort are remote.

> "Lord my God, I call for help by day;
> I cry at night before you. ...
> Let my prayer come into your presence.
> O turn your ear to my cry."
>
> *Psalm* 87(88):1&2

- ii   The inner deadness and fear of non-being.

> "I am reckoned as one in the tomb;
> I have reached the end of my strength,
> like one alone among the dead;
> like those you remember no more,
> cut off, as they are, from your hand."
>
> *Psalm* 87(88):5

- iii The hurt of rejection, being despised and not understood.

> "You have taken away my friends
> and have made me hateful in their sight."
>
> *Psalm* 87(88):8

Despite all this, the psalm is a persistent prayer showing that the pain must be worked at and faced before God's grace breaks through.

CHAPTER 2:5

DEFENSE MECHANISMS: THE HYSTERICAL DEFENSE

People who adopt this defense against facing their own inner pain are always extroverts. They need other people from whom to draw emotional energy and sustenance. They are therefore exhausting to be with and most people tend to distance or avoid them.

The nature of their inner pain is essentially one of emptiness. A gnawing emptiness and hunger for love that makes them feel so desperate that they believe that if they do not get it now, and in large amounts, they will perish by drifting into nothingness. The message they get from within the depths of their being is that 'all the love I need is in other people and if I do not do everything within my power to draw it off them, I will perish'. The message they give to other people is, keep away from them or else you will be sucked dry.

It is within these last two factors that the problem lies. What such people need they never really get, because no other person can give it in the quantity required. The hysterical defense is then operated by increasingly subtle and seductive manipulation of others, attention seeking and always being at the centre of everything. This ploy never satisfies because they never secure enough real love. In between the frantic activity that the attempts to secure love involve, comes bouts of gloom, darkness and deep despair; when the hysterical defense is exchanged briefly for the schizoid one. It is never however a thoroughly going schizoid mode, but more in the nature of a sulk after the manner of a petulant child. Those who adopt the hysterical defense pattern of behaviour are neither introvert or reflective enough to stay long in the schizoid defense. It is used as a short resting period and manipulative ploy in preparation for the next extrovert move.

The reasons why people become hysterical in their behaviour can be seen to come partly from their nature and partly from their nurture. The nurture they receive tends to be inadequate in two areas. The first area is that of mothering. They have not experienced enough accepting, nurturing love to make them feel an acceptable person just as they are. The second area of nurturing comes from fathering. I have observed in all such people an inadequacy in their father as a person. He is either absent or not caring, or weak and over-indulgent, not able to use wise discipline. I think this is why most people who adopt a hysterical defense respond very well to firm but consistent friendship and spiritual direction over a long period of time.

The nature of such people is extrovert and aggressive. Because they are extrovert they need other people to live through and being aggressive they go out and get them. This is the exact opposite of those who adopt schizoid defenses. The great weakness of this kind of extrovert, active, aggressive person is their lack of self-reflective ability. They feel their pain but do not understand it, and they look for solutions that will not work at all. They cannot build an ivory tower and find it most difficult to make even a small inner sanctuary in which to meet God.

But this last thing is what they need help to do. They need to meet the screaming, unloved child within, and give it to God to be loved. They need a friend who is firm and understanding and perhaps initially to meditate with them for a specific time on a regular basis. One who will be consistent and yet not get drawn

66

into extending the time little by little until the whole system breaks down and yet another rejection has to happen.

For those who recognise something of themselves here, Psalm 41(42) is very valuable. I offer is as a basis for meditation and prayer. May I, before doing so, say that many to whom this applies may not recognise it themselves at all, but those who do so are growing spiritually already by virtue of the fact of recognition. Nothing can be forced on people who are not ready. We just need to watch, pray, love and accept them as they are, looking to ourselves and our own emotional and spiritual sustenance as we do so.

Psalm 41(42) expresses the need to experience God's love in very strong and positively lustful ways. This is the basic need of those who adopt a hysterical defense. It expresses this graphically in the first two verses:

> "Like the deer that yearns
> for running streams,
> so my soul is yearning
> for you, my God.
>
> My soul is thirsting for God,
> the God of my life;
> when can I enter and see
> the face of God?"
>
> *Psalm* 41(42):1&2

These sensuous words are ones that express an inner need of love. They make spiritually sensuous and concrete in a way that appeals to the hysterical in people and should be meditated upon over and over again, feeling the cool refreshing water and imagining the loving face of God as shown in Christ. To do this in front of a good icon of Christ could be beneficial.

A later verse underlines the extrovert element in those who adopt the hysterical defense:

> "These things will I remember
> as I pour out my soul:
> how I would lead the rejoicing crowd
> into the house of God,
> amid cries of gladness and thanksgiving,
> the throng wild with joy."
>
> *Psalm* 41(42):4

The danger is that such people will only contact God through others and not direct. If God is not met in isolation, then when there is no festival or others are not present, God cannot be reached. The hysterical person sees prayer as more real and powerful with others in a prayer group; whereas the schizoid sees prayer in isolation from others more real and powerful. This is to do with one being extrovert and the other introvert. Whatever we are basically we need to live it out fully without denying it, but also give some time and effort to developing our opposite or shadow trait.

Finally, the refrain:

> "Why are you cast down, my soul,
> why groan within me?
> Hope in God; I will praise him still,
> my saviour and my God."
>
> *Psalm* 41(42):5&11

expresses both the pain (heaviness) of the hysterical person, and the source of healing.

The other statement that contributes to the heaviness is in the verse:

> "With cries that pierce me to the heart,
> my enemies revile me,
> saying to me all the day long:
> 'Where is your God?'"

Psalm 41(42):10

The hysterical person is very aware of their image, of what other people think about them and their beliefs. They need always to justify themselves and appear good in the eyes of others. The pain of not doing so is felt as deep rejection, 'that pierce me to the heart'. They even experience people who are schizoid in tendency as rejecting them when they are not.

CHAPTER 3:1

GODWARD ASPECT OF THE PSALMS: THE SPIRITUAL DIMENSION

Having taken some time looking at the human responses that are conditioned by our individual psychology, in the form of the defense mechanisms that are built up so that we can survive in a fallen world, it would seem wise to take a look at the Godward aspect of the psalms. Not to do this would imply that we are concerned only with a psychological understanding of their message. This would be most inadequate because although the psalms do contain many psychological insights, they also have a mysterious content which has been recognised throughout the ages by many saints and scholars. This mysterious aspect is their eternal other-worldliness. The voice of God speaking through them which builds up and sustains the individual's relationship with God and gives grace in understanding from a spiritual standpoint the politics of the world.

We begin with a psychological viewpoint because to begin with our individual responses and their distortions would seem to be Christian wisdom. It is based upon Our Lord's injunctions in Matthew 7:1-5 to clear our own vision first before looking at others.

> "Judge not, that you be not judged. For with the judgement you pronounce you will be judged, and the measure you give will be the measure you get. Why do you see the speck that is in your brother's eye, but do not notice the log that is in your own eye? Or how

71

can you say to your brother, 'Let me take the speck out of your eye', when there is a log in your own eye? You hypocrite, first take the log out of your own eye, and then you will see clearly to take the speck out of your brother's eye.''

When we have done this, then we can look outward towards others in a true spirit of love and humility.

The process of so doing however involves our relationship with God, the Godward aspect. This gives us the further insight required to discuss spiritual truths that are often hidden behind material and literal objects and facts. This is an issue the Christian Church has wrestled with continually throughout history, central, then to this is our spiritual life which centres upon our own relationship with God, to which we will now attend.

The tension between literal and allegorical (mystical) interpretation of scripture.
This has always existed, even in pre-Christian times, the Jewish Rabbis held to these two schools of thought when interpreting the scriptures.

The allegorical or mystical interpretation sees all scriptures as having a hidden spiritual meaning which only those who have been specially initiated can understand. The literal and historical aspect does not matter to those who are totally committed to this view. For them it does not matter if a miracle did or did not happen as recorded. What matters is what it teaches us about God and our spiritual life. Therefore, all who argue about the facts recorded do so because they do not have the spiritual ability, gift or whatever to grasp the real spiritual point.

The literal interpretation sees all scripture as describing what is literally true and has to be believed as such without question. For such people it is important always to show the literal truth as a fundamental part of their faith. The validity of their relationship with God depends on it, whereas for those who take the allegorical view, their relationship with God is a mystical reality verified by their own spiritual experience.

It seems to me that both of these views of scripture have a valid point to make, but both when taken on board completely to the exclusion of the other do violence to the true nature of scripture. In history the wholesale adoption of the allegorical view always leads to gnosticism and an unreal fantasy spiritual life, whereas the wholesale adoption of the literal view leads to either a rejection of the spiritual world as unreal, or a narrow strait-jacketed spiritual life which can neither relate with nor enrich the everyday world in which we all live.

Both extremes taken alone are not Christian in that at the centre of Christian faith is the Doctrine of the Incarnation, which claims that in Jesus Christ both the spiritual and material (mystical and literal) worlds are fused together. Both are equally important and they balance each other as part of a whole. This is why I used the word 'tension', because intellectually it is hard to hold two such apparently opposing truths together. In fact, purely as an act of the intellect, it is impossible. We can only do it through the disciplines of prayer and sacrament, and by the work of the Holy Spirit.

There are in scripture, literal historical facts recorded, there is also allegory, parable, poetry, prophesy and even things nobody seems to understand. No one theory will interpret them all and many will remain a mystery to us all our lives. Nevertheless, there is also the fact that the words of scripture over the centuries have spoken to people of all races in a way that feeds the

73

soul, strengthens faith and points to God. It is a way of speaking that I intend to examine because it is a fact of human experience well established, and the psalms have shown themselves to be an important factor in this.

God speaking through the psalms

Two examples only will I take from history because they reflect the experience of many.

Firstly, John Cassian (c. 400 A.D.), a monk who wrote on monastic life and the struggles individuals went through in developing their relationship with God, made the following statement: "The psalms teach us the true path to the spiritual understanding of scripture" (from: De Coenobiorum Institutis II vol. 49).

The spiritual understanding is that which feeds the soul and builds up faith. It involves using psalms in prayer and meditation so that through repetition of the words, mulling them over in the mind and asking God to speak through them we receive something of God from them. The psalms contain so much that is truly human as well as divine that everyone can relate their own experience to them. They help us to recognise and accept what is in us and when we can do this honestly, then a window to God is opened in our souls and we can see Him, not fully, but in glimpses which sustain us in faith.

In the previous chapters we have been concerned very much with seeing ourselves in the psalms, which is a necessary beginning to the process of the spiritual growth, that leads us to seeing and knowing God spiritually. Many people never get close to God because they never get close to knowing themselves as they truly are. We therefore have begun at the beginning, but now move on to that in the psalms which reveals God.

74

In so doing, we are automatically led on to all other scriptures, the psalms being our starting point. This brings us to the second example from history, chosen because it reflects a very wide experience of many people.

Thomas Merton, a monk of the twentieth century, points out that within the psalms Jesus is revealed to us if we have eyes to see him (from: Bread in the Wilderness p. 20)

"He, [Jesus Christ] is the word of God hidden in these 'words of God' [the *Psalms*]."

This again points to the mystery of the psalms. It shows also something important about the nature of God. It is that God is self-revealing and we must learn to respond to Him in such a way that we can receive what He is desiring to give us. Hence the earlier insistence on this work being an aid towards making an honest response to the psalms and to our own experience. By learning to respond honestly to the psalms we discover God who is behind the words.

This is where the literal and mystical come together. We begin by responding to the literal, the immediate, the words which stir us, and end up by experiencing a mystery beyond them. If, however, we become over concerned with, and bogged down in, a literal understanding, we do not get beyond it to the mystery of God, the living God. George Herbert (1593 - 1633) in his poem 'The Elixir', adequately expresses this:

"A man that looks on glasse
On it may stay his eye;
Or if he pleaseth through it passe,
And then the heav'n espie".

In the history of the Christian Church all the early Church Fathers saw Christ in the psalms. It is a standard Christian doctrine that the whole of the Old Testament points to Jesus Christ as Messiah, but the psalms were seen as that bit of the Old Testament most suitable and profitable for worship, liturgy and private meditation, necessary for feeding the soul. There were disputes amongst the Church Fathers as to which psalms contained Christ (i.e. were Messianic) and which were not, but all of them saw him in at least a handful.

The Psalms are strictly the property of the Jews, in wordly terms, but in content they belong to the whole human race. I always think how indebted we all are to the Jews every time I read them, but I also, as a Christian, see Jesus their Messiah revealed in them.

At this point it is appropriate that the psalms be allowed to speak for themselves. This is much more important than whether what I have just said by way of introduction is true or false. The following four psalms, 72(73), 84(85), 13(14), 52(53) are offered with some comment as being expressions of Godward aspect of the Psalm.

Psalm 72(73)

This Psalm is sometimes given the title 'The problem of innocent suffering'. It can be divided into three parts:
1:     Verses 1-14 which states the problem
2:     Verses 15-17 which show how the individual believer comes to terms with such an apparently bad and insoluble problem
3:     Verses 18-28, the results of the individual coming to terms with the problem.

This is a psalm that is concerned with practical faith for a thinking person. Let us now examine these three parts in more detail.

1:    The Problem
The problem is stated in verses 2 and 3

> v. 2   "Yet my feet came close to stumbling,
>   my steps had almost slipped
>
> v. 3   For I was filled with envy of the proud
>   when I saw how the wicked prosper."

The rest of this section elaborates verses 2 and 3. They point out that in this world wicked and selfish people ignore God and seem to get away with it. In materialistic terms they get the best jobs, influence people, become famous, tell lies that people believe; and all this leaves them healthy, wealthy, prosperous and their pride seems to pay dividends. In all this God is brushed aside and he seems to do nothing about it, whereas the Godly and faithful wonder if their way of living is futile, a mere illusion.

> v. 13   "How useless to keep my heart pure
>   and wash my hands in innocence,
>
> v. 14   when I was stricken all day long,
>   suffered punishment day after day."

2:    The solution
This proved beyond human ability, there is no rational solution to this problem;

v. 16 "I strove to fathom this problem
too hard for my mind to understand."

Here we see the limits of intellect in solving many problems and
the need for a higher source that is mysterious. One that comes
from God through his Holy Spirit.

v. 17 "Until I pierced the mysteries of God
and understand what becomes of the wicked."

It would seem that there has to be a spiritual dimension to
solving such problems and this involves breaking through into
the presence of God so that He can show us. This always
happens when, by his grace, we realize the limits of our own
understanding and seek Him in prayer.

The phrase translated from the Hebrew as "... until I pierced
the mysteries of God ..." could also be translated as "... until I
entered God's Holy Places ...". I find it interesting that the
plural of 'Holy Place' is used. The Holy of Holies in the temple
at Jerusalem was where man met God in the Old Testament
times, but in Christian times this was destroyed. At the crucifixion, the veil of the temple that contained the holy place was
torn:

"And behold, the curtain of the temple was torn in
two, from top to bottom; ..."

Matthew 27:51

Jesus was also heard to have spoken of destroying the temple
and building it in three days, referring not to the actual temple
building but to the temple of his body:

78

"... we heard him say, 'I will destroy this temple that is made with hands, and in three days I will build another, not made with hands.'"

Mark 14:58

Jesus is saying here that the temple he will build is a spiritual one not a building made of material. This could be thought of as referring to any of three 'temples': the Christian church at worship, the sacrament of the Eucharist, or the inner temple of the individual believer.

These are all 'temples', or holy places in which God meets people who believe in a spiritual way, and in which he communicates his truths to them. There are many other places in the gospels where this idea is developed; the idea that individual believers can meet spiritually with God in many places or situations, and God will communicate His truth to them. The whole of chapter 16 in John's gospel is relevant here and worth giving time to read and meditate upon; also the first Epistle of John chapter 3 and the gospel of Luke 24:13-35 (the road to Emmaus story).

In conclusion, Psalm 72(73) verse 17 is saying that only by entering regularly into the Holy Place God has created for us, and accepting the spiritual disciplines involved, will we ever be able to come to any satisfactory understanding of the world and its problems because the basis of them all is a spiritual one. Here the basic principle has been set out but later on other aspects of this will be examined.

3:    The outcome of coming to terms with the problem in a spiritual way
In short, the outcome is a wider awareness of the nature of

reality both within one's own self and in the world as a whole.

a: The outer reality in the world as a whole.
Verses 18-20 and verse 27 all state that the ungodly will not prosper ultimately.

> v. 18 "How slippery the paths on which you set them;
>   you make them slide to destruction.
> v. 19 How suddenly they come to ruin,
>   wiped out, destroyed by terrors.
> v. 20 Like a dream one wakes from, O Lord,
>   when you wake you dismiss them as phantoms
>
> v. 27 All those who abandon you shall perish;
>   you will destroy all those who are faithless."

They may appear to prosper short term; but the Godly, although they suffer, will survive. History has proved this over and over again. In this century alone, atheistic and tyrannical governments have come to an end - Hitler and Fascism, Stalin and Marxism (even though it took about 70 years to demonstrate its emptiness and begin to collapse). The apparently arrogant and prosperous people are set on a "slippery path" (verse 18). This, as has been said earlier, is the way of all who believe in the sufficiency of their own abilities. Why we often fail to see this is because we have too short a time scale. Like infants, most people want to see immediate results. Only spiritual maturity will give the correct time scale and only a deeply rooted Godliness will give us the patience to endure long enough to see God work. This is why the inner awareness of the reality of spiritual things is a sine qua non, as far as understanding the nature of the outer reality is concerned.

b: The inner awareness, Verses 21 and 22 are the key ones:

>   v. 21   "And so when my heart grew embittered
>   and when I was cut to the quick,
>   v. 22   I was stupid and did not understand,
>   no better than a beast in your sight."

All bitterness creates spiritual deadness and makes people vulnerable to living a level of life that creates and perpetuates evil. Those who have been hurt are nearly always made bitter by it. The natural response is to seek revenge and to this end the bitterness is fed, thereby destroying. Deliverance from this self-destructive trap of bitterness is a matter for spiritual action, a touch of God, which comes from entering "God's holy place" and experiencing his presence.

The need for this 'touch of God' and allowing God to heal the soul, so that a true justice can be brought about, is expressed in many other psalms, as is also the opposite; the result of turning from God to our own human resources and its consequent destructive outcome.

Psalm 93(94)

A prayer for God to vindicate. This is a good prayer for any who feel wronged, hurt and oppressed. It wisely asks God to act because the rulers of this world are inadequate in bringing about justice. It also guards the individual from the temptation to act from their own hurt and bitterness, thus making things worse.

Psalm 11(12) is a shorter psalm in the same vein and very helpful as a prayer.

Psalm 13(14) and 52(53)

These spell out the consequences of ignoring God, they both develop the words of Psalm 72(73) verses 21 and 22 quoted above. Their message is that when human beings lose contact with God and do not regularly meet with Him in his holy places, then they slowly become de-humanised. This is the greatest evil of atheism, its slow but sure way of de-humanising people. Both of these psalms begin with the same words:

> "The fool has said in his heart:
> 'There is no God above.'
> Their deeds are corrupt, depraved;
> not a good man is left."

Having said this, atheism is not the only way that a person can become corrupted. False spirituality and false religion can do the same, more will be said about how the psalms speak of this, next.

CHAPTER 3:2

GODWARD ASPECT OF THE PSALMS: FALSE SPIRITUALITY & FALSE RELIGION

Human beings are all basically spiritual beings; but because for the time being we live in a material world, a tension is created. The material aspect of our lives is more immediate, it touches us first more obviously. The satisfaction of material needs is more obvious and more immediately satisfying; it is also easier to handle, to explain and to understand. We are compelled by our earthly situation to 'go for it'; not to do so can leave us (in the immediate) cold, hungry, friendless and without status - in short, a most desperate failure.

Nevertheless, total and adequate material satisfaction on its own leaves an emptiness which only slowly makes itself felt, often in middle life. The early stirrings of the awareness of this emptiness, which is spiritual, in most cases drives people into a search for further material satisfaction to fill the space. This in turn gets people hooked on the law of diminishing returns - the more people have materially, the less satisfying it becomes and the more is then sought, and from this comes the conflict of striving to compete, to gain and to achieve.

This fundamentally materialistic struggle can become 'spiritualised' in a most subtle way and in the end it produces false religion and false spirituality. The attempt to fill the emptiness, without the pain of true conversion or real repentance that gets us in touch with the living God, is its basis.

- False Spirituality -

The roots of a false spirituality come from making God too small, reducing him to our size by projecting onto him our own images, ideas, hopes and aspirations. False spirituality is always infantile psychologically. It wants immediate results, has no patience, cannot endure hardship or uncertainty, needs everything to be available in simple form.

All of us wrestle with this if we are in a state of reasonable spiritual growth. Psalm 16(17) speaks of this and has been given the title 'Appeal of an upright man'. It describes the struggle for spiritual truth in this present world and ends with a very interesting statement:

> "As for me, in my justice I shall see your face
> and be filled, when I awake, with the sight of your
> glory."
>
> *Ps* 16(17):15

This psalm should be read and prayed alongside Paul's first letter to the Corinthians chapter 13. Both show the need for continued spiritual growth to take place in us throughout our whole life in this world, because we will not see God or understand him fully this side of the grave. We need his grace to do this which must be mediated in love.

> "For our knowledge is imperfect and our prophecy imperfect; but when the perfect comes, the imperfect will pass away. When I was a child, I spoke like a child, I thought like a child, I reasoned like a child; when I became a man, I gave up childish ways. For

now we see in a mirror dimly, but then face to face. Now I know in part; then I shall understand fully, even as I have been fully understood. So faith, hope, love abide, these three; but the greatest of these is love."

1 Cor. 13:9-13

A true spirituality is universal, it applies equally to all people. Psalm 86(87) states this and it is used here because it is one that can easily be misunderstood and interpreted in a materialistic way. It is a Messianic psalm and should be read alongside the gospel of John chapter 1 verses 1-18 and the Book of Revelation chapter 21 verses 1-7.

The term Sion used in psalm 86(87), God's Holy City, should be understood spiritually rather than materially. It speaks of God moving towards man from heaven and creating a place where all can meet and enjoy him as equals; not the establishment of an earthly kingdom in which one religion is dominant, be it a type of Judaism or a type of Christianity.

Much of spiritual value is said in the verses of this psalm. They are prophetic not only concerning the entry of Jesus into the world, both at a certain point in history as a man, but also his continued coming until the end of this world as a guide to all who seek God in truth:

"The true light the enlightens every man was coming into the world."

John 1:9

The risen ascended Messiah comes now in spirit to guide all who seek God in truth, but the fulfilment of the prophetic nature

85

of this psalm is still to come. Perhaps that is why it is so open to misinterpretation by us, who are so conditioned by this world in which everything should be explained now and completely.

The following apocalyptic vision of St. John (Book of Revelation) is the future fulfilment of Psalm 86(87) as stated in its last verses:

"In his register of peoples he writes:
'These are her children'
and while they dance they will sing:
'In you all find their home.'"

Ps 86(87):6-7

"After this I looked, and behold, a great multitude which no man could number, from every nation, from all tribes and peoples and tongues, standing before the throne and before the Lamb, clothed in white robes, with palm branches in their hands, and crying out with a loud voice, 'Salvation belongs to our God who sits upon the throne and to the Lamb!' And all the angels stood round the throne and round the elders and the four living creatures, and they fell on their faces before the throne worshipped God, saying, 'Amen! Blessing and glory and wisdom and thanksgiving and honour and power and might be to our God for ever! Amen.'

Then one of the elders addressed me, saying, 'Who are these, clothed in white robes, and whence have they come?' I said to them, 'Sir, you know'. And he said to me, 'These are they who have come out of the great tribulation; they have washed their robes and made them white in the blood of the Lamb.

Therefore are they before the throne of God,
and serve him day and night within his temple;
and he who sits upon the throne will shelter them with his presence.
They shall hunger no more, neither thirst any more;
the sun shall not strike them, nor any scorching heat.
For the Lamb in the midst of the throne will be their shepherd,
and he will guide them to springs of living water;
and God will wipe away every tear from their eyes.'''

Rev. 7:9-17

- False Religion

The two marks of false religion are that it is always strongly legalistic and very rational. It over-emphasises ethics at the expense of grace. It therefore puts burdens on people too heavy to bear, divides people and creates a superior class at the expense of the majority of people. It is always humourless and loveless.

The subtle thing about false religion is that it looks good from the outside and is appealing to the worst side of our nature. That side which seeks security through certainty, and having everything set out systematically so that there is an explanation for everything. It excludes mystery and therefore deceives. It creates evil by giving us the authority to act against evil to overcome it in such a way that it creates more evil.

The root cause of false religion lies in the materialisation of spiritual things. All denominations of the Christian church have been guilty of this at some time, but nearly always this has arisen out of a zeal for good, i.e. doing something practical to put things right. Psalm 48(49) speaks very prophetically of this.

The introduction to the theme of the psalm states that what is said is important for everyone, no exception is made, it is for all people. The message is not a simple statement. It is wisdom and insight. The intellect can cope with it only in the form of a parable. This shows the transcendent mystery of a problem that will be solved by using a harp:

> "My lips will speak words of wisdom.
> My heart is full of insight.
> I will turn my mind to a parable,
> with the harp I will solve my problem."
>
> *Psalm* 48(49):4-5

The use of a harp is important, it indicates the place of the arts rather than the sciences, (fine art, poetry, literature and music), in bringing about insights into life's meaning and even healing.
The next section of Psalm 48(49) is the message of the psalm, which is focused in the statement:

> "For no man can buy his own ransom,
> or pay a price to God for his life.
> The ransom of his soul is beyond him.
> He cannot buy life without end,
> nor avoid coming to the grave."
>
> *Psalm* 48(49):8-10

This message can be applied to several levels of life today.

One level is the purely materialistic which seems to say that with enough money everything can be solved. Scientific research can be funded which will find an answer to all our ills. This, in extreme, is an empty foolish faith. Its danger is that in part it contains truth, so much so that it can solve many problems. The easy life style and better physical health of advanced industrial societies show this. They have achieved much by creating wealth and using it to make life on earth more tolerable. But there is a cost which only makes itself felt slowly. Socially, it divides. The rich and clever in the end keep their comforts at the expense of the poor and less clever. Materially it destroys a limited environment, affluence creates effluent which poisons. Advances in a scientific materialistic approach to medicine create problems such as: drugs with side effects, antibiotics which create new kinds of immune bacteria, the keeping of dead people 'alive', and in some cases the fantasy that death can be avoided.

Failure then becomes a problem and not a means of growth, in such a materialistic environment. People are either winners or losers and that is not the nature of the vision expressed in Psalm 86(87) nor that of the apocalyptic vision of John. Spiritually this psalm and all associated scriptures, see the dividing line being between those who opt into life and those who opt out. This world's failures can be such because they have opted into a better spiritual life and therefore do not need this world's success. Jesus Christ took this line very much in the gospels.

From a materialistic world, if we are not careful we can get a materialistic religion that tries to pay God a price for our life. The price can be outward observances that ignore the inner reality. Valuing all materialistic expressions of religion, forgetting that Jesus Christ was born in a stable as a poor refugee child. It is only too easy to look for God in the wrong place, and this can be in a church building or organisation that He vacated long ago, leaving an empty materialistic shell, with heavy pressures on people to raise money to keep it going.

Modern therapies are also vulnerable to becoming false religions. Again we have the same problem that they do contain truth and they do help people. It is therefore easy for both therapists and those receiving therapy to become trapped by the very means of the help they value. Complete redemption is always beyond the therapy or the therapist, the helper and the helped. It lies within the bounds of the grace of God. That indefinable touch of God which is beyond all human ultimate control or understanding. This is the wisdom Psalm 48(49) offers us. It is repeated twice:

"In his riches man lacks wisdom:
he is like the beasts that are destroyed."
Psalm 48(49):13 & 21

In short, we are told that human riches, be they seen as money, power, status in society, cleverness, skills of all kinds, and intellectual ability; all have the power to reduce us to a foolishness that will destroy, because they can cut us off from the only source of wisdom which is God.

- Psalm 21(22)

This psalm is one of the definitely Messianic ones and should be read and compared with Isaiah Chapter 53. Jesus Christ used it as a prayer when he was dying on the cross and it goes more deeply into the suffering involved when the material world is set aside in order to pursue a spiritual path. This is not easy because it demands much more than the will or desire to reject the current values of the world in which we now live for spiritual ones; (even though one might be intellectually convinced that the spiritual life is best, is more rewarding in the end, and is eternal rather than transient).

The main reasons for the difficulties in following the spiritual path are:

i: It is lonely

"My God, my God why have you forsaken me?
You are far from my plea and the cry of my distress."
...'

Psalm 21(22):2

ii: It involves a suffering that cannot be borne in a state of loneliness because without affirmation we totally doubt ourselves, even our own existence,

"But I am a worm and no man,
the butt of men, laughing-stock of the people."

Psalm 21(22):7

and yet it often has to be borne in loneliness.

iii: The world we reject hits back at us very hard

"All who see me deride me.
They curl their lips, they toss their heads.
'He trusted in the Lord, let him save him;

let him release him if this is his friend.'

Yes, it was you who took me from the womb,
entrusted me to my mother's breast.
To you I was committed from my birth,
from my mother's womb you have been my God.
Do not leave me alone in my distress;
come close, there is no one else to help.

Many bulls have surrounded me,
fierce bulls of Bashan close me in.
Against me they open wide their jaws,
like lions, rending and roaring.

Like water I am poured out,
disjointed are all my bones.
My heart has become like wax,
it is melted within my breast.

Parched as burnt clay is my throat,
my tongue cleaves to my jaws.

Many dogs have surrounded me,
a band of the wicked beset me.
They tear holes in my hand and my feet
and lay me in the dust of death.

I can count every one of my bones.
These people stare at me and gloat;''

Psalm 21(22):8-18

iv: God does not seem to act in our favour at all but seems to continue ruling the earth from heaven in his own way:

"O my God, I call by day and you give no reply;
I call by night and I find no peace.

Yet you, O God, are holy,
enthroned on the praises of Israel."

Psalm 21(22):3-4

For the Christian who experiences these terrible things, the only positive factor is the knowledge that Jesus Christ suffered the same things and came through victorious. We trust also, and at times without concrete evidence in our own lives, that He is with us in spirit (see the gospel of *John* chapter 1 verse 9, and *Revelation* 7:9-17) and will bring us through sometime, either in this world or the next, we do not and cannot know when:

"So when they had come together, they asked him, 'Lord will you at this time restore the kingdom to Israel?' He said to them, 'It is not for you to know times or seasons which the Father has fixed by his own authority. But you shall receive power when the Holy Spirit has come upon you; and you shall be my witnesses in Jerusalem and in all Judea and Samaria and to the end of the earth.'"

Acts of the Apostles 1:6-8

At this stage it is useful to make a reference to Psalm 93(94) because it refers to one very important issue. It is a strong desire, even overpowering urge, to act on our own behalf to put things right and bring about justice and revenge.

This works in very few cases. Mostly it makes matters worse and creates more evil. Most issues in which we have been hurt or offended can only be put right in a real way by God acting. This psalm says this and the first two verses should be made a prayer in all such cases.

> "O Lord, avenging God,
> avenging God, appear!
> Judge of the earth, arise,
> give the proud what they deserve!"
>
> *Psalm* 93(94):1-2

It is wise to be very reluctant to take action unless we are very sure it is totally within our power to achieve a just end. By praying this psalm we can see much more that is positively achieved, and even receive some inspiration from God on occasions when we are called to act:

> "Will he who trains nations, not punish?
> Will he who teaches men, not have knowledge?"
>
> *Psalm* 93(94):10

Finally, in this chapter on the Godward aspect of the psalms it is appropriate that the inward aspect of our spiritual life be balanced with an outward look towards God. Praise and adoration of Him is important, not only in public worship but as a response to God's glory grace and love, as and when we experience it in our everyday living. There are many psalms suitable as vehicles for this, but I wish to recommend Psalms 144(145), 145(146) and 146(147).

Turning outwards in praise is essential for spiritual health, not only because it prevents the negative aspects of too much introspection, but also because it is a defense against getting trapped by Satan. Some people get too bothered by Satan, others deny his existence, especially when he has already blinded them.

Spiritual health involves renouncing the devil and all his works. We do this practically not by just looking away from him. This only creates a vacuum. We do it by turning positively towards God in praise regularly, and training ourselves to do it on every possible occasion.

CHAPTER 4:1

SELECTED HUMAN PREDICAMENTS: BEING LET DOWN BY THOSE IN WHOM WE TRUSTED

Relationships

It is a very important part of living a fully human life that we should enjoy, and be sustained by, intimate relationships with other human beings. Many people suffer because they either do not have such relationships, or have had them and they went wrong. In many cases, the failure of a relationship has been of such magnitude that it has left the individual so hurt and afraid of intimacy that no other close relationship is ever attempted; hence the schizoid reaction which has been mentioned earlier.

This experience of failure can turn people towards God and away from people, but it can also turn them away from all relationships. When either of these happen, the result is that the person is left diminished, and their life is made spiritually and emotionally barren. A good and fruitful relationship with God also needs relationships with other people; for a relationship with another person to be full and balanced, a relationship with God is important. Which of these two relationships comes first is hard to say, they are both so interdependent.

A very hurt person, deprived of human love, might find enough to keep them going through a direct experience of God's grace; but they will be operating in a very withdrawn religious life-style. Sooner or later there often emerges within them a longing for human relationships, an intimate soulmate or just a relaxing friend.

On the other hand, some equally hurt people cannot make the

direct link with God. They need an understanding human relationship to prepare the way, a physical human presence that has a spiritual quality and, as it were, shows the human face of God.

These two factors in relationships both have their own dangers. The person who has a direct experience of God can be stuck in an inadequate relationship with Him; this because they are never stimulated into seeing Him more fully as reflected through others. Those who strongly need and use other people can: either, get stuck at a human level, demand more of human beings than they can give and end up being abandoned by them; or they can make human beings into minor Gods, thereby depriving themselves of the fullness of God in all His riches.

Throughout the psalms much is said about relationships of all kinds, but here the intention is to look at only two psalms because they say something about close, intimate relationships.

These close intimate relationships can be divided into two kinds. The first kind are those essential to our basic nature, development and patterning. The second are peer group relationships made in later life when we have some degree of maturity. These peer relationships can be termed as being sustaining relationships, whereas the first kind are best described as nurturing relationships. Although this differentiation is made, it is mostly for the necessity of making a point of importance in an attempt to achieve some clarity. In practice, both kinds share much in common and overlap each other in a way that makes discerning between the two quite difficult.

Nurturing relationships

These are basically the relationships we have as small undeveloped children, with our parents. They set up patterns of relating to others; when adequate, they help us to grow into adulthood, and make good sustaining relationships with others. Where they are not adequate, or set us patterns of relating that are not balanced, we carry them over into poor adult relationships. These poor relationships are those whose essential nature is that of sustenance, a dependant need of being nurtured that can diminish the mutuality of the relationship.

Sustaining relationships

These are the relationships between peers. They have a high degree of mutuality and are in essence supportive. They enrich both people equally and can be very intimate and beneficial for our wellbeing.

The two psalms we are now going to look at are about these kinds of relationships going wrong; they are offered as a basis for meditation to people who suffer this way.

Psalm 26(27) for those whose parents have not adequately nurtured them:

This is sometimes called 'a psalm of triumphant trust in God' - an apt name because it speaks of a faith in God that overcomes abandonment by mother and father, but it also still retains echoes of that abandonment; this is very true to most people's experience. Even when the grace of God has given a healing of supernatural dimension; in those who have suffered there is always some emotional deprivation from early infancy, an underlying fear of a new abandonment that lurks like a ghost in the depths of their being.

Verses 1-6

These verses are an affirmative song of praise to God for what He has done. They have a ring of great confidence in Him and are therefore very important for use by those who have suffered abandonment, they are a means of strengthening faith by turning the mind outwards from self towards God.

Verses 7-10

In this section all the old fears of abandonment come up to the surface to haunt the once abandoned but now healed person. In these fears past ghosts haunt the mind of the one of new found trust; possible stirred up by the activity of Satan.

With the prayer to God not to abandon as mother and father once did, comes a most interesting and repeated plea to "seek his face". For an infant the most comforting object is the loving face of mother. This need is still there and transferred to God. Together with the pleas: "Dismiss not your servant in anger" and "do not abandon or forsake me", we see the painful images of a bad parent being projected onto God. This is a very important aspect of healing, but it must be done honestly and full-bloodedly, not in a mild whimpering born out of a false piety.

Verses 11-14

These verses move the process of healing on to a further stage with the words: "Instruct me Lord in your way; on an even path lead me". This takes us into an adult frame of mind, so essential for spiritual growth and progress. Too many people want to stick in their babyhood faith; this is not a very good tendency because in the end it destroys that which God once gave. Verses 13 and 14 point us on towards God in a way that is hopefully realistic:

"I am sure I shall see the Lord's goodness

in the land of the living
Hope in him, hold firm and take heart
Hope in the Lord''

We cannot look back as Lot's wife did, because our faith will die. Instead of becoming more fully human we could become a pillar of salt (metaphorically speaking!). In the gospel of Luke 17:33 and 34, Our Lord refers to the wife of Lot who looked back towards Sodom and Gomorrah as they fled from the doomed cities (Genesis 19:1-29) and was changed into a pillar of salt. He uses this to illustrate a point about faith; namely, that it involves moving onwards, and it is only too easy to destroy it by looking back (in the wrong way) on that which we should have left behind.

By looking back negatively to that which is in the past, it can still have power to destroy us. This is very true of emotional hurts. They paralysed us when they first happened, and if they are not put away now, can still paralyse our faith to live fully in the present.

Psalm 54(55) for those who have been let down by a close friend:

This psalm is sometimes given the title 'Distress of a man betrayed by his friend'. It expresses a wide range of feelings experienced by such people, and finally turns to God as being both trustworthy and the ultimate vindicator of those who have been hurt in this way. This psalm ends on the theme that Psalm 93(94) takes up and develops: namely, that in those most damaging and hurtful of situations in which there appears to be no human hope of redress, God alone can heal, vindicate and restore.

This psalm can be divided into three sections, each one dealing with a different aspect of the problem of being let down in a relationship that was a mutually sustaining one.

The first section deals with feelings aroused in such a situation: the second one states the facts of the case. The third one starts with a short but strong emotional outburst at the point where the horribleness of the let-down and its implications are fully realised; but it ends with a statement about faith in God at a point where trust in people breaks down. Let us now look at these three sections in a little more detail.

Verses 1-12

The first two verses plead with God for attention. When let down by other people, doubts about God and his reliability, or even existence are raised. This is a very human emotional reaction and has within it the roots of atheism. Especially severe are those feelings of abandonment if first felt in infancy as a result of inadequate parenting, and they repeat themselves most strongly when a let-down is experienced again in adulthood. From verse 4 onwards the emotions expressed are basically fear of being overwhelmed and destroyed, especially verses 5 and 6:

> "My heart is stricken within me,
> death's terror is on me,
> trembling and fear fall upon me
> and horror overwhelms me."

v. 5&6

Ways of coping with these feelings are also expressed. The first one is the paranoid defense of projecting it all onto others.

In verse 4 it is the foe, the person who is an enemy, who brings all this pain. In fact the whole world is full of them, they are everywhere, the city and its streets are full of them, nowhere is free from tyranny and deceit:

"Night and day they patrol
high on the city walls.
It is full of wickedness and evil;
it is full of sin.
Its streets are never free
from tyranny and deceit."

v. 11&12

The second way of coping that is expressed is the schizoid one, a way that involves switching off or rising above it:

"O that I had wings like a dove
to fly away and be at rest.
So I would escape far away
and take refuge in the desert."

V. 7&8

Verses 13-15
This could be called the turning point simply because pain that had been seen and felt generally (no doubt because it was all mixed up with pain from previous hurts) is now pinpointed and seen specifically. These three verses state this precisely:

"If this had been done by an enemy
I could bear his taunts.
If a rival had risen against me,

103

I could hide from him.
But it is you, my own companion,
my intimate friend!
(How close was the friendship between us)
We walked together in harmony
in the house of God."

vv. 13, 14, 15

It is always a stage forward in the healing and coping process when pain can be seen and accepted within the framework of the here and now of our existence. It can then be confronted more realistically. This is the basic principle of Gestalt Therapy; in the psalms it marks the turning point from being in a general state of fear, pain and agony (about which one can only rant, rage and lash out at others), to being in a situation in which one can take responsibility for oneself and receive grace.

Verses 16 to the end

This last part shows how the process of turning to God for grace and healing takes place following the process of coming to a specific awareness of the situation that caused the hurt. A realistic assessment of our human situation always makes us aware of our need of God's grace. Truth in the inward parts of our being always predisposes a person towards a living faith. A living faith on its part helps us get a clearer view of reality; but these things never come smoothly and in a totally unclouded way. Hence the outburst in verse 16:

"May death fall suddenly upon them!
Let them go to the grave:
for wickedness dwells in their homes

and deep in their hearts."

v 16

followed by the statement in verse 19:

"He will deliver my soul in peace
in the attack against me:
for those who fight me are many,"

v 19

and the repeat of this pattern in verses 21, 22, 23

"The traitor has turned against his friends;
he has broken his word.
His speech is softer than butter,
but war is in his heart.
His words are smoother than oil,
but they are naked swords."

v 21, 22, 23

The last section of the psalm shows well how the emotions of the Godly person ebb and flow like the tide, totally controlled by a force outside itself. This happens whenever they are touched by suffering inflicted upon them from other people who, in most cases, show outward signs of wickedness.

The ebb is when all balance, inner calm and reasonableness drain away and strong vindictive emotions take over. These are then projected onto the 'ungodly', or whoever is perceived as being the enemy. Sometimes these 'ungodly' are really bad and evil, sometimes no worse than most of us; there can be times when they are totally innocent of whatever is being projected onto them:

> "The traitor has turned against his friends,
> he has broken his word"

v 21

The flow is when the Holy Spirit seems to touch the inmost being of the afflicted, it results in the opposite to the ebb of Godly feelings:

> "He will deliver my soul in peace"

v 19

and the very last verse of the psalm

> "O Lord I will trust in you".

This psalm tells us what we are really like and is a deliverance from false piety if meditated upon genuinely. It shows how an ebb and flow of emotions does not destroy faith, cut us off from God, or permanently destroy our inner peace. It is, in fact, essential that we allow it to happen because it is to do with living fully in this present world in a relationship with God that is honest. When other people hurt and upset us, we should moan to God about it, pouring out to Him all our worst thoughts and feelings. We should do this in a whole hearted and full-blooded way; then, when we have emptied ourselves, His Spirit can flow into us to heal and restore. Only then can we with integrity make the final statement of this psalm:

> "O Lord I will trust in you."

CHAPTER 4:2

SELECTED HUMAN PREDICAMENTS: THE SHOAH
- A BEREAVEMENT EXPERIENCE

Introduction

This work is part of an overall examination of the therapeutic use of the psalms: the effect of using them to express to God exactly how we feel (in good times and bad). As the psalms were first created by the Jewish people at times of heightened emotion, it seems relevant to examine the most traumatic Jewish experience of this century, that of the Holocaust (or the 'Shoah' - destruction, desolation - as many prefer to call it). It seems sadly appropriate at this time (January 1991, at the beginning of the Gulf War), when Jews once again find themselves in direct fear of holocaust and death by poison gas, that our minds are turned once again to an examination of the relationship between the Jew and his seemingly (to the Gentile) silent God. There is some justification in seeing the whole Holocaust experience in terms of a prolonged grief process - a drawn-out bereavement; it is in this light that the experience will be examined.

It is not the purpose of this work to examine why there were those who really believed that the spiritual life of the world would be improved by the destruction of the synagogues, the burning of the books of Torah and Talmud, the prohibiting of the practices of Sabbath and Festivals, and (in the 'Final Solution'), the elimination of every single Jew in Europe. Nor is it the purpose of the work to describe the systematic destruction of the life of the Jews of Europe, and detail the horrors of the

107

Holocaust.

It does seem relevant to ask whether survivors (and, indeed, non-survivors) of this appalling time (Shoah) found that the use of prayer helped at all, or whether they felt able to express to God what they felt about their situation by the use of psalms, or in other ways, or not at all. What evidence exists that the psalms were used at this time by both ordinary people and in a formal liturgical way? Were certain, specific lines of the psalms used in times of stress or emotion?

Of course, just as any study of the effect of the threat of holocaust and gas on Jews at this time (the 1991 Gulf War) would be incomplete without a sensitivity to their memory of the holocaust experience; so, a study of the holocaust would be incomplete without reference to their collective memory of other destruction experiences. Though one who has never been through Shoah can never fully enter into the experiences of the survivors (and the non-survivors), there is enough common ground to attempt a tentative appreciation of the dreadful trauma to which one group of men subjected another - persecution, alienation, herding into ghettos, transportation in trucks, appalling ill-treatment in camps, and finally gassing and burning.

To examine the process of bereavement and grief experienced in the Shoah, it is first necessary to outline the normal process of grieving and then to link this to the Jewish experience.

Bereavement: a natural process of re-adjustment

Grief is a natural process involving a number of emotions. Bereavement (whether of a person, a lifestyle or even a well-loved object) is painful and traumatic; when the trauma is fully experienced and worked through, then healing can take place and emotional health restored. This emotional re-adjustment can be long and drawn out, but if time and space is allowed for it, then healing and peace of mind will be the final outcome. If grieving does not take place, then the result is emotional imbalance, and the ability to cope with life becomes very restricted. The grieving process of the Jews at that time was complicated by the fact that the bereavement was so massive, it involved their whole way of life; the grieving was also made more difficult because it extended over such a long period of time and each bereavement was compounded by another; usually they simply did not have enough energy or time to grieve. (This incomplete grieving will be examined further at a later stage.)

During grieving it is very important for emotional health that every emotion experienced is expressed, whether it be despair, anger or simply the need for helpless tears. It is reassuring to say with the psalmist:

> "Those who are sowing in tears
> will sing when they reap.
> They go out, they go out, full of tears,
> ...
> they come back, they come back, full of song,
> ..."

Psalm 125(126)

Bereavement: the stages of grieving

The normal process of grieving seems to have recognisable and well-defined stages; while, however, the vague outlines of stages can be seen in most people, the process does not have the same

109

neat orderliness in everyone. It is usually chaotic with the stages running into each other, sometimes people jump a stage or revert to an earlier one on the way towards a later one. The whole process, if allowed to run its course, normally takes about two years.

Bereavement: the first stage, shock, denial, isolation

In a normal bereavement experience, the first stage in the process of grieving seems to show the immediate symptoms of shock, denial and isolation. We are all familiar with the normal response to sudden or bad news: "No, it's not true; he can't be dead, you've got it wrong, I only saw him this morning, he was OK then" - the first stage at the onset is denial: the grieving person will not admit that the worst has happened; in the case of a death the actual death is denied. As far as the Nazi persecution was concerned, when the first news of the death camps filtered through to the Jewish communities, they could not admit to the truth of the reports; when they were rounded up themselves, they stood in shock not believing what was happening to them.

In normal times, when the initial denial is overcome then a period of isolation follows: "Leave me alone; I want to be by myself" is the cry of a newly-bereaved person, they isolate themselves from contact with others and sit for hours staring into space. Photographs taken of groups of Jews being herded into ghettos or onto transport trucks show shocked bewildered people each locked in a private hell of their own; accounts tell of people marching doggedly to the ghettos or the camps, unquestioning, chanting the normal prayers and psalms for a journey:

"May it be thy will O Lord our God and God of our fathers, to conduct us in peace, direct our steps in peace ... to deliver us from every enemy, ambush and hurt by the way ..."

prayer

"He who dwells in the shelter of the Most High
and abides in the shade of the Almighty
...
Upon you no evil will fall,
no plague approach where you dwell"

Psalm 90(91)

"Thou are my shelter; thou wilt preserve me from trouble ... may the King answer us on the day when we call ..."

prayer

"I lift up my eyes to the mountains:
from where shall come my help?
My help shall come from the Lord
who made heaven and earth.
...
The Lord will guard your going and coming
both now and for ever"

Psalm 120(121)

There must have been comfort in the chanting of the familiar prayers and psalms; still a sense that God would protect them, even denial that evil things could not, and were not, touching them. Only when they reached a destination and the reality began to impinge on their frozen minds did they throw their bags to the ground, sink down and pray the familiar prayer of their liturgy:

"Oh God, Lord of the Universe take pity upon us in Thy great mercy".

Bereavement: the second state, longing and searching (anger or apathy)

As the denial wears away and the need for isolation decreases, the phase of longing and searching begins. At this stage pining, crying and a feeling of emptiness predominates, there is much talking about the loss. Two subsidiary reactions can take place - anger and apathy; either one or the other of these two reactions can take place on their own or in some cases they both happen alternating with each other.

The first reaction - anger - may be violent anger, rage and protest; the grieving person has great outbursts or anger, blaming all sorts of people and situations for what has happened, sometimes even blaming themselves. Often when a death occurs, we hear the bereaved person say: "It's the doctor's fault, he should have diagnosed it sooner" or "I should never have let her go out, it's all my fault". It was natural for the Jews, faced with the horror of the death camps, to experience times of anger. At the first sight of the crematory, as flames were leaping up, they did not want to know what was burning. Then there was the gradual realisation that the load a lorry was delivering was little children, babies; they saw with their own eyes the children in the flames. Someone began to recite the Kaddish, the prayer for the dead; the prayer was recited for the children and as realisation of the reality of the death camps grew, others joined in and the emphasis of the prayer changed - people began to recite the 'prayer for the dead' for themselves:

> "May His Name be blessed and magnified ..."
>
> *prayer*

It must have been while chanting prayers such as these that the anger would well up in their hearts; anger against the God in whom they had put their trust:

> "For the first time I felt revolt rise up in me. Why should I bless His name? The Eternal, Lord of the Universe, All-Powerful and Terrible, was silent. What had I to thank him for?"
>
> 'Night' - Elie Weisel

But the question a Gentile might ask: "Now, where is God?" would be answered by Jews: "God is here in this experience, in this part of our history".

> "The three victims [two adults and a child] mounted [the gallows] ... 'Long live liberty!' cried the two adults. But the child was silent. 'Where is God? Where is He?' someone behind me asked ... [Later] the two adults were no longer alive ... being so light, the child was still alive ... 'Where is God now?' And I heard a voice within me answer him: 'Where is He? Here He is - He is hanging here on this gallows...'"
>
> 'Night' - Elie Wiesel

113

Throughout their experience, Jews maintain that God himself has entered his people and is actually present in their history. There is a difference of emphasis in the theology of salvation; the traditional Christian - heavily influenced by Greek philosophy - tends to see salvation in terms of the freeing of the mind and spirit from the body, (a body subject to death and decay), and from his earthy history; Jews place no such emphasis on the body-mind split - God is in him in his entirety and in his history however dreadful it may be. The question: "Where was God?" should rather be: "Where were their fellow men?" It was not God who abandoned his chosen race but rather man who had alienated his fellow man. Not that the Jews absolved God of his part in all this destruction and pain; the Jew, bolder than his Christian brother, hurled accusations against his God. Emboldened by the knowledge that he is the one chosen by God, his robust faith allows him to address God as an accuser - both he and his God are covenanted to each other for all ages - as his anger and rage are expressed to God, a closeness develops which enables him in some way to enter the mind of his God and begin to understand:

"As for me Lord, I call to you for help:
in the morning my prayer comes before you.
Lord, why do you reject me?
Why do you hide your face?"

Psalm 86(87)

The other possible reaction at this 'longing and searching' stage is withdrawal into apathy or depression: a feeling that life is not worth living, the loss has made everything valueless and nothing will ever be satisfactory again. The bereaved person says: "Now he's dead I have nothing to live for". There are many accounts of the phenomenon of the *'muselmänner'* (musselmans) - those amongst the inmates of the death camps who, too tired to understand, fell into total apathy and drowned in despair; those with drooped head and curved shoulders who lost touch with their fellow inmates, the living dead whose only destination was the gas chamber:

> "Their life is short, but their number is endless; they, the Muselmänner, the drowned, form the backbone of the camp, an anonymous mass, continually renewed and always identical, of non-men who march and labour in silence, the divine spark dead within them, already too empty to really suffer."
>
> *'If this is a man'* - Primo Levi

They might have found strength if their weary souls had been capable of calling to mind the words of the psalm:

> "The enemy pursues my soul;
> he has crushed my life to the ground;
> he has made me dwell in darkness
> like the dead, long forgotten.
> Therefore my spirit fails;
> my heart is numb within me.
> ...
> In the morning let me know your love
> for I put my trust in you.
> Make me know the way I should walk:
> to you I lift up my soul."
>
> *Psalm* 142(143)

For others in the death camps, as they faced once again the elimination of yet another fellow Jew, the depression was mixed with the feeling of isolation usually experienced in the first stage of mourning:

> "Those absent no longer touched even the surface of our memories ... The instincts of self-preservation, of self-defence, of pride, had all deserted us. In one ultimate moment of lucidity it seemed to me that we were damned souls wandering through space till the generations of man came to an end, seeking their redemption, seeking oblivion - without hope of finding it."
>
> *'Night'* - Elie Wiesel

Bereavement: the third stage, mitigation and bargaining

As the longing and searching is worked through, a phase of mitigation begins; the sufferer begins to come to terms with what has happened. In cases of death, some people have illusions of seeing or hearing the beloved one who is lost: "I still hear his footsteps on the stairs". It is at this stage that some people try to 'hold on' to the deceased by various means thus preventing themselves from moving on to the next stage of grieving. Those in the camps who clung on to their past found it disintegrating around them; they themselves began to disintegrate too. Those who could not let go of an inadequate theology, or an inadequate concept of God, began to lose faith altogether - at the first signs of cracks in their faith structure they lost their reason for struggling and began to die. For the most part, as far as the survivors were concerned, the degree of religious faith was not affected by the experiences in the camps:

"As with many survivors ... the degree of his religious faith was not affected by the concentration camp experience ... Those who did believe before the camps in general continued to; those who were mildly or conventionally religious quite frequently lost their faith; those who had no faith did not gain it through the camps."

'Journey back from Hell' - Anton Gill

It is arguable that those believers who lost their faith were those who lost their reason for living and became like the *'muselmänner'* destined only for the gas chambers - and so were not counted among the survivors.

During this third stage, some sufferers go through a kind of bargaining process, they try putting some explanation forward with the idea that the creation of certain circumstances will put it all right. There are always those who will slip into superstition, those who will frantically chant their prayers as if using them as magic spells: "Father in Heaven, may your name be praised" turns from a prayer of faith and love to a somewhat cabbalistic chant of appeasement. There were some in the camps who turned to the Cabbala for comfort; they looked for signs and interpreted verses of the psalms by use of numerology, some claimed to predict the end of the war or the coming of the Messiah. At the time of the slaughter of Jews in Poland three centuries before, they had clung to the belief that just before the Messiah comes there will be an era of great disaster, then they prayed, fasted and did penance in an effort to hasten the coming of the Messiah. There were some in the death camps who also saw the twentieth century disaster as the prelude to the coming of the Messiah or at least to the coming of the Kingdom; some looked towards the building up of the Jewish state (the state of Israel):

> "By the rivers of Babylon
> there we sat and wept,
> remembering Sion
>
> ...
> O how could we sing
> the song of the Lord
> on alien soil"
>
> *Psalm* 136(137)

Bereavement: the final stage, acceptance and letting go

In the final stage of grieving - acceptance - there is a gradual gaining of a new identity. The grieving person begins to 'let go' of the dead person. It is the end of the emotional process and the only point at which it is possible to discuss rationally with the grieving person any practical plans for coming to terms with the loss and building a new life.

As part of the letting go process the place of death rites and rituals is important: throughout time and all over the world, man has celebrated death with some sort of ceremony. The ritual of committing the body to the ground or to the fire is an important rite of transition for the grieving person. As with any ritual, it reduces anxiety by making some sort of order out of an otherwise chaotic situation; it also offers support by showing the grieving person that they are not alone but a member of a supportive group. In a public act two changes are marked. The bereaved act out their change in social status (a married woman officially becomes a widow, a child officially becomes an orphan). The deceased officially receives the status of one who is going on the journey to the next life. The various rituals have the function of making it easier for the grieving person to 'let go' of the dead one. For those grieving, it reduces anxiety about what happens to the dead person: prayers or exhortations over the body serve as good wishes for a journey, this is consoling for those who worry that the journey may be a difficult one; prayers also give reassurance to those who fear that the dead may not 'rest in peace'. Another important function of the funeral rite is the expression of support for the bereaved, they are no longer mourning alone but are part of a group who have 'been there before' and have survived. The Jewish liturgy encompasses a burial service, prayers for use in the house of the mourner, prayers for the setting of a tomb stone, and memorial services of the dead for use on anniversaries and feasts; all make varied use of the psalms. In the burial service the saying of *Psalm* 15(16) reassures the mourners about the fate of the departed (and soothes the anxieties of those who are worrying about their own fate):

"I say to the Lord: 'You are my God,
My happiness lies in you alone

...

even my body shall rest in safety.
For you will not leave my soul among the dead,
not let your beloved know decay"

Psalm 15(16)

During the holocaust, although there are many accounts of the Kaddish (prayer for the dead) being recited both over individual bodies and as part of the normal liturgy still performed in the camps, there was still a great need felt to ritualise the deaths of so many counted and uncounted who had been unceremonially buried or burned. When the last death camp had been liberated, the last count made, when the number of Jews slaughtered had risen from one million to three million to six million, the ritualised mourning of the dead and the letting go could begin in earnest.

Unfinished, inadequate, and delayed grieving

There are many factors which can prevent the total working through of the bereavement process; lack of time and energy, the effects of previously unresolved grief, longstanding psychological problems, inadequate concepts of death, lack of 'space' in which to express emotions, ...

The grieving process of the Jews at that time was complicated by the fact that the bereavement was so massive; not only did they lose family and friends but they also lost their homes, their countries, their possessions, familiar religious objects which were so important to their life structure, and their whole way of life. The grieving was also made more difficult because it extended over such a long period of time; each bereavement was compounded by another - just as they began to come to terms with one change, then another would occur. Their experiences at this time triggered off memories of the many times in the past that their race had lived through similar traumas; the Hasidic Jews had strong and powerful memories of the slaughter of their forefathers in Eastern Europe, all had the accounts of their race's history from scripture to draw on. Jews have a history of being scattered, of living in the gaps between others' spaces, of having to be tenants. Experiencing alienation from those around them, they have had to find their 'home' in their separate lifestyle and culture, their security in the knowledge that they are the chosen of God. It is for this reason that, as they make their collective pilgrimage through the ages, they have continually reinforced feelings of rejection and alienation. These systemic feelings of rejection are projected onto God in some of the psalms used in the liturgy:

> "Yet now you [God] have rejected us, disgraced us:
> you no longer march with our armies.
> You make us retreat from the foe
> and our enemies plunder us at will.
> You make us as sheep for the slaughter
> and scatter us among the nations.
> You sell your own people for nothing
> and make no profit by the sale."
>
> *Psalm* 43(44)

To grieve properly takes time and enough space to work through the various stages to full emotional health; often, in everyday life there are more pressing matters which can distract from this process. Unless time and space is allowed for the process to be followed through, re-adjustment can never take place and full emotional health cannot be re-attained. Those who were in the death camps had more urgent drains on their psychological resources; the day to day necessity to ensure their own immediate survival drained them of energy to grieve. Those without enough

121

energy to work through the first two stages of grieving were often those who were simply unable to continue the day to day fight for life and became counted among the non-survivors. Those who survived spent years working through their grief; many never did manage to come to terms with the experience, many became emotionally stuck at one or other of the bereavement stages.

For adequate bereavement, a balanced theological concept of death is required. It is spiritually incomplete to deny the importance of this present life in an effort to over-emphasise the wonders of the life to come. The physical absence of a loved one is a very real absence, it is a denial of the pain of the loss to rejoice too soon in their immortality. True, they are now with God; but belief in heaven should in no way be a substitute for going through the painful process of bereavement and so coming to a real re-adjustment to life without the loved one. A true theological concept of death embraces the importance of life and creation, and the reason for our very existence. Those who go through the pain of re-adjustment become spiritually stronger and gain a more real understanding of the mind of God; thus becoming closer to Him. Those who deny their pain are never able to grieve, they risk becoming unfeeling both to themselves and to others. There is no doubt that the spiritual resources exist within the Jewish faith for a good understanding of death, the liturgical resources are also there in the form of the varied prayers and services for the dead; much has already been said about the chanting of the Kaddish. Those in the camps who were able to deny their pain as a means of survival, though they may have seemed unfeeling, were often those who coped at the time and were counted among the survivors; unless they did their grieving later they never regained their ability to fully experience pain of the love of God and of fellow man.

The importance of expressing the various emotions has been already stressed. At each stage a different emotion is experienced, sometimes several emotions are felt together, often it is difficult to separate out the different feelings: a need to cry may be mixed with a need to hit out in anger. When the emotions are expressed (either in private or in the company of others), then the bereaved is able to move onwards. When emotions are not expressed, the bereaved is unable to move past that emotion, they will go through life unable to properly re-adjust. There is no doubt that emotions were expressed at times in the camps; life was so basic that basic emotions were expressed often in a very raw form. It was the brave survivor who managed to recount, in an unsanitised way, some of the more real feelings he experienced during that time; when the real struggle for life ensued then the emotions were raw and uncensored. In a sense, it was because life was such a struggle that raw emotions were brought to the surface uncensored; this may have helped sustain the emotional health of the survivors. Those who were unable to admit to their baser emotions became full of shame and unable to look fully at their experience and to work it through; part of their past became locked away. It is interesting to see how basic the emotions are which are expressed in the psalms; the chanting of the psalms often helps to unlock those emotions hidden by those who are ashamed of them.

For those who already have unresolved emotional problems (or psychological disorders) when bereavement strikes; their grief triggers off all sorts of unresolved problems, these problems get mixed up in the grief process thus making it complex and difficult to handle. Those with an underlying neurotic problem will become more neurotic (those with depressive leanings get locked into depression; those who suffer from paranoia become more paranoid...); the psychopath will exhibit his usual psychopathic tendencies. These people need help to unravel their underlying problems. Those in this category who survived the camps may well have had their behaviour contained by the day to day structures; on release, they were left with both their original problem and their unresolved grief. Many never became psychologically whole; each subsequent bereavement triggered off unresolved memories.

For a bereaved person, the loss of a loved one often shows up the quality of the relationship they had with them. It is difficult for people to admit to the quality of their relationships, often it is not even examined; but those with unsatisfactory relationships usually have difficulty in grieving for the lost one. Mourning can take the form of a continual unconscious searching for them or even the creation of a shrine to them; in this way the bereaved becomes locked in the past and unable to enjoy the opportunities of the present. Unsatisfactory relationships with people, with things, with beliefs, with places ... can all be mourned in this way. 'Exiles' often create shrines to their old homeland and to their old religion which become more real to them than their actual surroundings; such practices have the possibility of becoming very morbid.

The effects of unresolved and incomplete grieving

Unresolved grief has the habit of re-emerging and hitting us between the eyes when we least expect it! Ordinary everyday sights, sounds, and especially smells, can trigger off unwanted memories. New bereavements can cause the re-emergence of the pain of old losses, the process of working through the old loss can suddenly begin again. The emotions involved with any of the stages of the unworked-through bereavement can re-emerge; behaviour patterns caused by the inability to pass through one of the stages can be psychologically limiting.

For some, trapped in the first stage of bereavement, the denial became a way of life. In later years they would neither talk about their experiences nor mix with other Jews, in the fear that the memories would surface. Some denied their Jewishness and took on a whole new persona, all their energy spent in eliminating traces of their past. For some, their past re-emerged as they faced later trauma or death.

For those whose mourning stopped at the second stage, anger or despair re-appeared when a further bereavement occurred. There were some (seemingly well-adjusted) who were suddenly plunged into despair years later; unexpected suicides were not uncommon. Inappropriate anger could surface in the face of seemingly trivial incidents.

When the letting-go process was incomplete, 'shrines' were created. The need for ritualised mourning by the use of prayers, of writings, of photographs, and of monuments, is still being felt today so long after the Shoah days; for some the ritualised mourning process is still necessary, the need to build shrines still there. There are those who wish to see the places of Shoah - Auschwitz, Bergen-Belsen, Dachau, Ravensbruch, Sobibor, Theresienstadt, Treblinka, ... - left untouched as monuments of shame; there are those who wish to sanitise them or even to erase the memory. There are those who wish to try to change the atmosphere of them by prayer; whatever their motive, the powerful words of the Chief Rabbi of France in our time should be heard:

"No one has the right to transform into a place of prayer this place [Auschwitz] where the most appalling idolatry was practised by man proclaiming the death of God and striving to make himself divine by reducing other creatures to the condition of objects, non-persons. Such prayers risk becoming in biblical terms, 'an abomination'. Auschwitz must absolutely become a place of absolute silence, non-prayer, non-testimony, evidence of paroxysm and havoc ... Let us all, together, make ours the words of the Psalmist. 'For you, Lord, the silence alone is prayer.'"

Chief Rabbi of France 1990

Another result of incomplete 'letting go' is the need to 're-place' what is lost: as the camps were liberated, many survivors felt a need to 'replace' their partly-mourned loved ones; there was a great urge to marry and reproduce. Many of these marriages were marriages of despair; children were born and named after a lost loved one, they were then expected to take on the burden of becoming an idealised replacement. These children were in a sense a 'shrine' to the dead, never able to live up the their parent's expectations and never able to understand why they failed. The problem of the unresolved grief of the survivors became the problem of the second generation and, in turn, of their families.

Years after the liberation of the camps, each new disappointment was capable of causing a re-enacting of the trauma of Shoah: whether the disappointment was death, divorce, illness, separation or even the loss of a familiar article. There are many who expressed uncontrollable and inappropriate grief when they broke a simple everyday article, a cup or a plate. Many found human relationships, with the possibility of disappointment, simply too painful - the risk was too great. Many went through life avoiding situations which might remind them of their loss; many limited their lifestyles and restricted their relationships with others.

Healing

Surprisingly, by the grace of God, many worked through their grief and became strong. By expressing to God their real feelings, they worked through the stages of grieving to a real and fuller relationship with God and with their fellow man. Not that they forgot their experiences, but they came to terms with them and became fully integrated people ready to ensure the continuity of the Jewish lifestyle. God had formed a covenant with them and entrusted them with a pilgrimage, and a promise of homecoming: they, in their turn, looked to their part of the covenant and were faithful to it. Throughout time, and throughout the world there were (and will always be) those who, threatened by the claim that the Jews are God's chosen people, seek to destroy the Jewish way of life. The survivors of Shoah are a testimony to the inner strength of man, healed people looking to the future but continually coming to terms with the past.

There are many survivors who once again faced, in a very powerful way, their nightmares; in Israel at the start of the Gulf War (1991) when the threat of poison gas once again became real. All sorts of unresolved memories must have flooded the minds of the holocaust survivors as they went, with their children, their grandchildren, and their great grandchildren into their specially sealed room; as they taped up the door after them, placed wet towels across the bottom of the door and then put on their hot uncomfortable gas masks. What they were doing must have seemed barely believable; their collective memory of the Shoah years must have weighed heavily as the process was repeated simultaneously in every home in the country. Flashbacks of earlier trauma must have been replayed as they saw toddlers being helped into cumbersome plastic breathing hoods, and mothers placing their babies in protective plastic tents. They must have remembered the experiments carried out on babies in the camps as they heard of babies being born and being transferred directly from their mother's bodies to anti-gas tents. The isolation and claustrophobia of the sealed room must have produced feelings of fear and helplessness, and evoked memories long since forgotten. They must have relived the feelings of insecurity experienced in earlier times, as they wondered if the truth was being held from them. Maybe they felt anger at the incongruity of the radio announcer's greeting to them as they sat in their sealed room at the start of the Sabbath: '*Shabat Shalom*'.

It is a tribute to the strength of these remarkable survivors that so many did manage to work through their grief. It is also a tribute to the many rabbis, doctors, psychologists and psychiatrists who worked and prayed with those who found the readjustment difficult, that so many were helped to come to terms with their trauma.

Did their relationship with God help them to come to terms with their pain? There is no doubt that through prayer many were put in touch with their emotions; many found God in their anger, many found Him in the familiarity of their everyday prayers. Some tried to hide from a real relationship with God by unfeeling chanting of liturgy; but eventually found healing through tears when suddenly struck by a phrase or sentence.

Maybe the process of grieving will never completely end, Shoah is part of the collective experience of the Jews, never to be forgotten. But even if the grieving were to cease and even if man were to forget the experiences of Shoah; God would remember, for God remembered His people in times of destruction in the past. After the flood God remembered Noah, He renewed His covenant with His people and showed them the rainbow as a sign for the future. Each time God remembers - a remembrance not for the destruction and hopelessness of the past, but a remembrance for the survivors and for their future.

EPILOGUE

What has been offered in this book is incomplete, this is because we live in a world that is incomplete. Within life a mysterious purpose is being worked out; mysterious, because it is only ever partly understood by us. Nevertheless, it does have an onward movement towards an eventual supernatural completion, and as a consequence, is beyond human control. Within this framework, human beings do have a limited amount of power. They can destroy large parts of the creation, themselves and each other. They can thwart the good purposes of God, and quite often the consequences of their own bad behaviour rebound back on themselves.

The psalms show all these things; they point us towards God who reveals himself to those who have spiritual eyes to see and ears to hear. God also reveals to us our own nature, if we are willing to see ourselves in His light:

"In you is the source of life
and in your light we see light"

Psalm 35(36):10

God also gives us grace to live a very practical life that can be worked out step by step, a day at a time, in a relationship of trust in Him. He does not deliver us from catastrophe and suffering, but He does give us grace to live through it and survive. He gives us both grace to survive, and a realistic hope that there is a better world to come, even though we may not fully understand it.

It is hoped that these insights and comments on the psalms

will help people who wish to enter on this pilgrimage of faith; that is the sole purpose. The aim not to ask you to agree or disagree, that approach is not the one called for. The purpose is to stimulate you to make your own pilgrimage and discover your own insights, from the use of the psalms in response to what is offered here.

The spiritual pilgrimage:

Most of the time on your spiritual pilgrimage will be spent just plodding on in hope. Sometimes you will experience great pain and discouragement and become negative in your outlook, believing everything to be hopeless. There will also be times when miraculously God breaks through and everything looks wonderful. You can also have fleeting glimpses of heaven that transform everything. None of these three states of being last for ever, they are part of the emotional flow of life and need to be accepted as such. The words of St. Paul express this:

"... I have learned, in whatever state I am, to be content. I know how to be abased, and I know how to abound; in any and all circumstances I have learned the secret of facing plenty and hunger, abundance and want. I can do all things in him who strengthens me."
Paul's letter to the Philippians 4:11-14

A life based on trust in God is not one that is smooth and easy. In the psalms we will find a true expression for whatever situation we are in at the time, but in this world it will never be a permanent one.

As we have already indicated, pilgrimage involves movement onwards. Our concept of God is therefore never fixed, in this world it is always inadequate. As we move on towards Him we will begin to understand different facets of His being and should slowly see Him more clearly as He is; but in this world we must always avoid the dogmatism that comes from believing that we have arrived. Those in this situation have in fact stopped moving and are spiritually bogged down, Psalm 16(17) and Paul's first letter to the Corinthians, chapter 13, express this well. It is an important spiritual truth.

Finally, two important needs are: true humility and the fellowship of others. True humility is knowing and accepting ourselves as we really are. To come to this is a slow and painful process, but it is essential if we are to be truly a person of faith. There are two ways in which this can happen and both are equally important; they must happen alongside each other and in interaction with each other. The one way is by our own prayer, meditation and self-reflection, and the other is by keeping the right company. That is, sharing our lives with people of integrity, in whom we can trust. Psalm 17(18) is relevant here, (especially verses 26-30):

> "You are loving with those who love you:
> you show yourself perfect with the perfect.
>
> With the sincere you show yourself sincere,
> but the cunning you outdo in cunning.
> For you save a humble people
> but humble the eyes that are proud.
>
> You, O Lord, are my lamp,

my God who lightens my darkness.
With you I can break through any barrier,
with my God I can scale any wall."

Psalm 17(18):26-30

May your pilgrimage be a fruitful one.